GL BAL FINANCIAL CRISIS AND CHALLENGES FOR CHINA

ALSO BY YANG MU

China's Industrial Development — Meeting the Challenges of the Post-economic Crisis Era (with Yu Hong)

China's Future: the Challenges for China's Economy in next Ten Years (with John Wong) (in Chinese)

China's Rural Entrepreneurs (with John Wong and Rong Ma)

Research on Industrial Policy (in Chinese)

Research on Industrial Policy in different countries in the World (with Zhou Shulian) (in Chinese)

Research on China's Industrial policy (with Zhou Shulian) (in Chinese)

ALSO BY MICHAEL HENG

Supply Chain Management: Issues in the New Era of Collaboration and Competition (with William Wang and Patrick Chau)

Destructive Creativity of Wall Street and the East Asian Response (with Lim Tai Wei)

State and Secularism — Perspectives from Asia (with Ten Chin Liew)

The Great Recession — history, ideology, hubris and nemesis

GL BAL
FINANCIAL
CRISIS AND
CHALLENGES
FOR CHINA

YANG Mu
Michael HENG Siam-Heng

East Asian Institute, National University of Singapore, Singapore

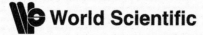 **World Scientific**

NEW JERSEY · LONDON · SINGAPORE · BEIJING · SHANGHAI · HONG KONG · TAIPEI · CHENNAI

Published by

World Scientific Publishing Co. Pte. Ltd.

5 Toh Tuck Link, Singapore 596224

USA office: 27 Warren Street, Suite 401-402, Hackensack, NJ 07601

UK office: 57 Shelton Street, Covent Garden, London WC2H 9HE

Library of Congress Cataloging-in-Publication Data
Yang, Mu.
  Global financial crisis and challenges for China / Yang Mu, Michael Heng Siam-Heng.
    p. cm.
  ISBN 978-9814282277 -- ISBN 9814282278
  1. Global Financial Crisis, 2008–2009. 2. China--Economic conditions--2000–
3. China--Foreign relations. I. Heng, Michael S. H., 1948–   II. Title.
  HB37172008 .Y36 2012
  330.951--dc23
                           2012016538

British Library Cataloguing-in-Publication Data
A catalogue record for this book is available from the British Library.

In-house Editor: Lum Pui Yee

Typeset by Stallion Press
Email: enquiries@stallionpress.com

Printed in Singapore by World Scientific Printers.

Preface

The rise of China has become a hot topic that has captured the imagination of the public, the business community and the political circles. Some commentators go so far as to say that it may well prove to be the defining economic and geopolitical change of our time. We reckon this is a gross exaggeration, for to do so is to neglect the impressive performances of other emerging economies and the resilient potentials of the advanced industrial powers. But it is fair to describe the economic rise of China as an important global event in the past three decades and the coming decades.

One important marker in this period is the bursting of the super-bubble in the global financial market in 2008. We write this book as an endeavor to look at the diverse implications the crisis has had and can have on the Chinese economy and some of its neighbors. In 2011, China moved ahead of Japan to become the second largest global economy. Does this imply that there is not much China can learn from Japan? This is an interesting question we explore in the book, which has broader relevance in developmental economics. What about the experiences of other countries, and the often murky discussion on the Washington Consensus and Beijing Consensus? We devote two chapters to these two inter-related questions.

Another question is the greater mutual dependence of China and its economic partners in Southeast Asia. The advent of the crisis has prompted the economic integration of these two economic regions to proceed faster, if not smoothly too.

Other questions are the debate on the exchange rates of the Chinese currency and the move to turn Shanghai into an international financial centre.

The above are the questions that are examined in the book. Earlier versions of some of the chapters have appeared as conference paper, journal paper, or as op-ed piece in newspaper. We are very aware that the topic is very vast, and there is no way we can hope to do justice to the study of it in one volume.

We would like to acknowledge our intellectual debts to our colleagues at the East Asian Institute who shared generously their insights with us, and to journal reviewers and conference participants whose comments helped us to present our ideas. The East Asian Institute has provided us with a conducive environment to do our research and writing, for which we are grateful. Finally we would like to thank Ms Lum Pui Yee, desk editor of World Scientific Publishing, who skillfully guided us.

Yang Mu and Michael Heng Siam-Heng
East Asian Institute
National University of Singapore
September 2011

Contents

Chapter One

Introduction

This book examines a few key aspects of the Chinese economy in the aftermath of the financial crisis. Before the crisis, the economy was growing at breakneck speed. The success story can be told in terms of economic reform guided by pragmatism, stepwise introduction of a free market economy, accession to the World Trade Organization, an industrial policy geared towards export promotion and selective learning of experiences from other countries. The Chinese economy has weathered a major political upheaval in the form of the Tiananmen incident of 1989 and a major economic storm in the form of the Asian financial crisis of 1997. What is even more significant is that it has managed to emerge from the 2008 global financial crisis in good shape. But as anyone with a sense of history would caution: past success is no guarantee of future success.

Three years have passed since the 2008 financial crisis. How has the Chinese economy fared during this period? China has responded to the shortfall with fiscal and monetary stimuli, and the results so far have been positive. In so doing, it has been able to make up for the weaker demand in the Western markets.

With this as the background, what has been the salient feature of the impact of the crisis? Speaking in a general sense, there is both change and continuity. The elements of change tend to appear in the news headlines. For example, we are told time and again that there is a shift in the centre of gravity of global economic power from the West. The G8 has been replaced by the G20. The International Monetary Fund has conceded that the emerging economies deserve to have a bigger say in the running of the Fund.

The changes are certainly important; so are the continuities. In terms of per capita income at purchasing power parity, China is ranked 94th, far below many other countries.[1] This is visible to any visitor who cares to

---

[1] List of countries by GDP (PPP) per capita, http://en.wikipedia.org/wiki/List_of_countries_by_GDP_(PPP)_per_capita [accessed 17 May 2011].

venture deep into the inner regions. There is still a big swathe of poverty. Bearing this in mind, it is easy to understand why the Beijing leadership shunned an active global leadership role in dealing with the impact of the global financial crisis. It repeatedly explained that the best way for it to play a positive role was to run its economy well. In so doing, China would provide a market for others' products. Continuing what it has done since the Asian financial crisis, it has increased its economic integration with the ASEAN countries with the implementation of the China-ASEAN Free Trade Agreement in early 2010. While this is certainly a move in the right direction, China could also try to reduce global imbalances by investing in productive assets abroad and buying high technology. In the face of American refusal to sell the kind of high technology that China wants and its attempt to block China's purchase of American assets, China can think of creative solutions to these problems.

Interestingly, another aspect of continuity is that the crisis was an occasion for the Western countries to raise an old issue with the Beijing government. They complained about their trade deficits with China and exerted extra pressure on China to revise its exchange rate upwards. They accused China of using its exchange rate as a mechanism to boost its exports while continuing to build up an unprecedented huge amount of foreign exchange. China has consistently denied the charge of currency manipulation. Related to this debate on the Chinese yuan is liberalization of the financial market. China's control of the currency flow has acted as a shield against the gales sweeping through financial systems in times of crisis. But as the Chinese economy grows to become the second largest economy and as it becomes more integrated into the global economy, the issue of financial liberalization looms larger. The issue is getting more urgent as China is gradually permitting use of the yuan as an international currency for trade and investment.

China has adapted the Japanese model since the early days of economic reform. But with the Japanese economy mired in two decades of recession, are there still useful insights to draw from the Japanese experience? Looking at the gap between Japan and China, one obvious answer is that China has yet to nurture and grow the Chinese equivalents of Mitsubishi, Toyota and the like.

Because China has also cherry-picked lessons from other East Asian countries, its development trajectory has not been a simple copy of Japan's. This has inspired some foreign observers to describe China's experience as the Chinese model. One of them even coined the term "Beijing Consensus" to capture the idea. Interestingly, the Chinese leadership and its leading economists have consistently denied that there is a Chinese development model. They seem more comfortable saying that they have been learning as they go along — citing the famous instruction of Deng Xiaoping of crossing the river by feeling the stones — and would prefer that other countries seek their own path of developing their economies. The BRICS countries, Indonesia and Turkey are emergent economic powers, all chalking up impressive growth in the aftermath of the financial crisis. Their people may say, "We live in an interesting time." It is not wrong for them to feel that their economies and societies are undergoing a particularly fascinating period. Between them, their experiences can certainly be distilled to add to the body of knowledge of developmental economics.

Chinese economists are deeply concerned with the issue of future growth. The impressive economic growth has been achieved on the back of massive investment, cheap labour whose supply is dwindling, depletion of natural resources and environmental degradation. Certainly, this approach is not sustainable.

Currently, the two most urgent issues are inflation and debts incurred by local governments. Inflation requires the government to adopt restrictive economic policies or at least to pull back expansionary measures. Investment is hampered by huge debts incurred by local governments and the current concern over rising inflation. As a result, the economic growth may not be big enough to generate the employment needed to maintain social stability. It raises the question of whether China is entering a period of stagflation with Chinese characteristics.[2] Meanwhile, it has proved difficult to stimulate private consumption, which remains in the doldrums because of the high cost of housing and weak social welfare system.

The economic problems facing China in the years ahead are quite clear to most China watchers. What is not clear is how these problems can be overcome. As students of social studies, we do not wish to make predictions. What we can perhaps offer is a discussion of some of the relevant issues, as a tool to help understand them.

The Rest of the Book

Chapter Two looks at the state of the Chinese economy amidst the global financial crisis. The economy has demonstrated its ability to hold up despite being badly battered by the crisis. The resilience is to a large extent due to

---

[2]Yang Mu and Yao Jielu, "Stagflation with Chinese Characteristics", EAI Background Brief, National University of Singapore, 2011.

its sound fundamentals. Despite having been able to successfully adopt an export-oriented approach for economic growth, the Chinese economy is also fuelled by its huge domestic demand. As a result, by increasing domestic demand through government spending, China has been able to cushion the full impact of the financial crisis. However, for the Chinese economy to retain its resilience in the future, there is a need for certain revisions in its structure. These include moving the economy up the value-added production chain and increasing the contribution of domestic consumption to the country's domestic demand.

Chapter Three discusses China's plan to transform Shanghai into a major international financial centre, on par with Hong Kong, Singapore, New York and London by 2020. The plan was announced in March 2009 by China's State Council. It was a timely move as it came at a time when China was assuming a greater role in global economic affairs. Indeed, China has replaced Japan as the second largest economy in the world. It is also the world's largest manufacturing base and the biggest commodity importer. Besides holding 40 percent of the world's foreign exchange reserves, it has the world's top three banks in terms of market capitalization. In 2009, the country accounted for 47.8 percent of the total value of IPOs worldwide. It is becoming bolder in the internationalization of its currency and is actively exploring means to reduce its dependency on the US dollar.

Chapter Four dwells on the yuan debate. The USA and Europe claimed that China had been deliberately maintaining a cheap Chinese currency as a means to boost its exports, to the detriment of their trade balance with China. With deep interdependencies between the USA and China, a cheap yuan benefits certain sectors in both countries, just as a revalued currency would benefit other groups in the two countries.

A key problem is America's huge trade deficit with China. It can be reduced if US companies sell what Chinese companies wish to buy. But Washington restricts such sales. A way out is for Chinese firms to buy European technologies and assets. With the money, European companies can buy American technologies and assets. This will reduce global imbalances and the dollar will recover, providing a benign environment for growth in the real economy.

Chapter Five discusses the China-ASEAN Free Trade Agreement (CAFTA) which was implemented in January 2010. It marks an important milestone in the relations between China and ASEAN. CAFTA builds on and extends the growing economic relationships between the two sides. The agreement is expected to further promote China-ASEAN trade alongside intra-regional direct investment and extra-regional FDI. However, as a result of the 2008 financial crisis, global economic conditions have changed significantly from those prevailing at the time of drafting the agreement. This may represent new opportunities and challenges. Its future success depends on how its signatory members can work together to overcome the challenges and make good use of the opportunities. Further down the road, ASEAN and China can build on CAFTA to enhance their economic cooperation and integration through coordination in monetary and fiscal policies as well as industrial policies.

Chapter Six examines the main features of the Japanese economic model and to what extent it still offers useful insights. In the 1950s Japan embarked on an export-driven developmental path that came to be known as the flying geese model. By the 1950s, many had noticed the success of the model and it was subsequently adopted by other East Asian countries. They too enjoyed decades of remarkable economic growth. An important element of the model is growth driven by exports to the USA and Europe. The bursting of the financial bubble in 1990 and Japan's subsequent response hold lessons for China. As a result of the 2008 financial crisis, the traditional markets of the "geese" are shrinking. The new situation poses grave challenges to both the existing flying geese economies and the latecomer economies which wish to follow the model. However, there remains much for China to learn from Japan in nurturing non-state-owned transnational companies able to compete successfully in the global market.

Chapter Seven looks at the renewed interest in economic developmental models in the wake of the 2008 financial crisis and the subsequent recession. News reports and commentaries highlight the Washington Consensus and the Beijing Consensus. Why has the Beijing Consensus enjoyed lukewarm reception among Chinese policy makers and intellectuals? Unlike a model designed for natural sciences applications, an economic model needs to consider the context of its application. Looking ahead, China may find it useful to study the experiences of the Nordic countries. They are able to combine social security with economic dynamism; they have low income disparity, low crime rates, high standards of living, good healthcare and they show concern for the environment.

Chapter Eight is the concluding chapter. It emphasizes the importance of sticking to the basics of creating economic wealth in the face of competition ideas such as value adding, productivity, production cost, innovation and efficient use of natural resources. These are ideas that apply to any economy and country. But any broad study of the Chinese economy would be inadequate without considering its continental size, both in terms of its geography and population. Its size allows China to try out different sets of industrial policies at the same time. It can follow the policy of nurturing *chaebol*-like transnational companies *and* the policy of supporting small and medium-sized enterprises. The chapter also offers a strategy to turn into a virtuous cycle the vicious cycle of persistent and rampant corruption, abuse of power, waste and social unrest.

Chapter Two

The 2008 Financial Crisis and the Chinese Economy

The global financial crisis has had a devastating effect on the world economy. Not only has it raised high levels of doubt on the fundamentals and sustainability of the current global financial system, it has also wiped out the euphoria that came with the strong growth posted by most economies in 2007 and early 2008. China is one good example. Prior to the outbreak of the crisis in the third quarter of 2008, China's economy had been expanding at a spectacular pace, registering double-digit growth since 2005. At one point, China's stellar economy even seemed to be overheating, prompting Beijing to introduce a series of measures to constrict economic growth. However, the onset of the financial crisis turned the tide as plunging world demand sent China's all-powerful economy into a downward spiral. Initially, the damage seemed to be extensive but as the world economy began to stabilize in 2009 and the huge stimulus package unveiled by Beijing took effect, China's economic situation improved. By the end of May 2009, green shoots of recovery seemed to have sprouted in China's economy, as illustrated by the stabilization of the decline in China's exports and the sharp increase in bank loans. Indeed, China's economy registered a strong growth of nearly 8 percent at the end of the second quarter of 2009. Whether these are real signs of recovery remains to be seen but they revealed the resilience of China's economy and the potential role of domestic demand.

The objective of this chapter is to explain the state of the Chinese economy amid the global financial crisis. It argues that the Chinese economy seems to be holding up despite being badly battered by the financial crisis. The resilience that the Chinese economy is showing is to a large extent due to its sound fundamentals. Despite having been able to successfully adopt an export-oriented approach for economic growth, the Chinese economy is also fuelled by its huge domestic demand. As a result, by increasing domestic demand through government spending, China is able to cushion the full impact of the financial crisis. However, for the Chinese economy to retain its resilience in the post-financial crisis world, there is a need for certain revisions in its structure. These may include moving the economy up the value-added production chain and increasing the contribution of domestic consumption to the country's domestic demand.

Effects of the Global Financial Crisis on China's Economy

China's red-hot economy slowed considerably as a result of the global financial crisis. In the final quarter of 2008, the Chinese economy registered one of its slowest growths of 6.8 percent. This pulled down economic growth for the whole of 2008 to 9 percent, ending China's nearly four years of double-digit growth. This continued well into the first quarter of 2009 as the Chinese economy registered a growth of only 6.1 percent. The slump generated a high level of uncertainty in China about whether the economy would be able to register a crucial growth of 8 percent for 2009, a level commonly regarded as the minimum growth rate to generate sufficient employment. But as 2009 progressed, especially after China posted a 7.9 percent growth in the second quarter of 2009, sentiments about the Chinese economy began to improve (Figure 2.1).

The weakness displayed by China's economy in late 2008 and early 2009 was attributed to the sharp drop in global demand for electronics, cell phones, steel products and other goods made or assembled in China. To a large extent, this was caused by the credit squeeze due to the outbreak of the subprime crisis in late 2007, which later manifested as a global financial

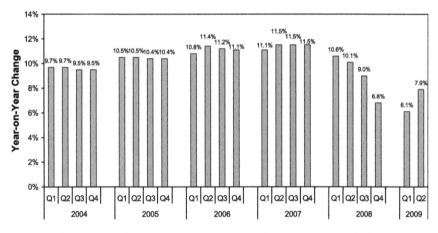

Figure 2.1.   China's quarterly GDP growth, Q1 2004 to Q2 2009.

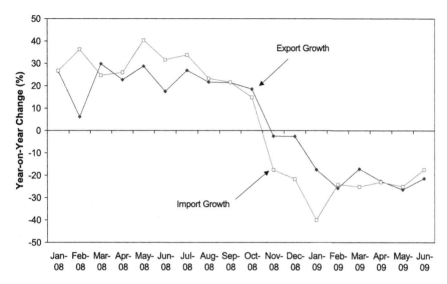

Figure 2.2.   China's trade growth, January 2008 to June 2009.
Source: Various compilations by the authors.

turmoil after the collapse of Lehman Brothers in September 2008. Indeed, China's exports had been in decline since the beginning of 2008 but it was after November 2008 that the plunge began (Figure 2.2). From November 2008 to May 2009, Chinese exports were falling at a year-on-year average rate of 20 percent in value. While the slide seems to have stabilized after the massive drop in February 2009 of 17.5 percent, the recovery of global demand is still largely dependent on the easing of the tight credit market.

As for now, global demand remains weak as banks in developed Western economies are still struggling to restore the credit market. It is crucial for global demand to recover, as a continuation of weak exports could force more Chinese factories to close down. Official reports show that at least 67,000 small and medium-sized companies across China were forced to shut down in 2008 due to inflationary pressure in the first half of 2008, followed by the retreat of global demand in the later half.[1] For instance, China's toy industry started the year 2008 with more than 8,600 factories producing and exporting 70 percent of the world's toys. But by the end of 2008, only about 4,400 remained.[2]

---

[1] "Factories Shut, China Workers are Suffering", *New York Times*, 13 November 2008.
[2] "Half of China's Toy Factories Close after Exports Slump", *The Times*, 10 February 2009.

The closure of Chinese factories has adverse effects on China and the global economy. For the global economy, the slowing down of China's industrial sector has led to a sharp decrease in Chinese demand for the global supply of equipment, machines and commodities such as crude oil and metals. From November 2008 to June 2009, China's imports slumped on a monthly average of over 25 percent in year-on-year value. While this could decrease China's trade surplus with industrialized economies such as the United States and the European Union, China's trade balance with regional economies may be affected.

In China, the rate of factory closures is driving the country's unemployment rate upwards for the first time since China began its double-digit growth in 2005. For instance, in February 2009, the Central Rural Work Leading Group stated that more than 20 million migrant workers had lost their jobs during the final months of 2008.[3] This was about 15 percent of the total migrant labour pool. According to the Ministry of Human Resources and Social Security, China's unemployment rate hit 4.2 percent at the end of January 2009, up from 4 percent in 2008. By the end of 2009, the Ministry estimated China's unemployment rate would reach 4.6 percent, the highest since the 1980s.[4] But this could be an understatement as the figure does not include migrant workers and university graduates.

According to *Beijing Evening News*, China would witness the graduation of 6.1 million students in 2009, the largest in history and nearly six times as many as in 2000. The figure is expected to increase to about 8 million in 2010 and 9 million in 2011. Beijing has implemented a number of measures to cushion the blow for unemployed graduates, such as providing loans for them to start their own business, encouraging them to take up government posts in rural areas and absorbing them into the Communist Party. However, these measures are still not generating enough employment opportunities due to the overwhelming number of graduates.[5]

Optimism Amid the Slowdown: Domestic Demand as a Source of Growth

Despite the bleak economic outlook, Beijing remains optimistic. During his "trip of confidence" to Europe in late January 2009, Chinese Premier Wen Jiabao stated in his speech at the World Economic Forum that he

---

[3] "Chinese Migrant Job Losses Mount", *BBC News*, 2 February 2009.
[4] "China's Unemployment Rate Climbs", *China Daily*, 21 January 2009.
[5] "Where Will All the Students Go?", *The Economist*, 8 April 2009.

expected China's economy to continue its growth amid the global downturn, including hitting the 8 percent target.[6] Premier Wen's upbeat outlook, however, contradicted the International Monetary Fund's (IMF) initial outlook of China's economy as it only predicted the country's economy to grow by 6.7 percent in 2009. But judging from the performance of China's economy during the period between the fourth quarter of 2008 and the first quarter of 2009, when the impact of the global financial crisis was the most severe, the Chinese premier's positive tone does not seem too far-fetched.

Indeed, in comparison with other Asian economies, China's economy seems to be holding up despite being badly hit by the financial crisis. Although China's GDP declined from 9 percent to 6.8 percent in the final two quarters of 2008 and then to 6.1 percent in the first quarter of 2009, China's overall economic performance during this period was still much better than its neighbours' as most of them registered record contractions during the same period (Figure 2.3). It is therefore interesting to highlight that China's economy was able to show such a degree of resilience despite facing a similar rate of decline in exports as its neighbours (Figure 2.4).

One explanation for the resilience displayed by the Chinese economy is that China's current economic slump is partly self-inflicted, as part of the process of the country's economic fluctuation or "business cycle". In the later part of 2007 and early 2008, the Chinese economy was in danger of overheating. The economy was clocking double-digit growth and investment

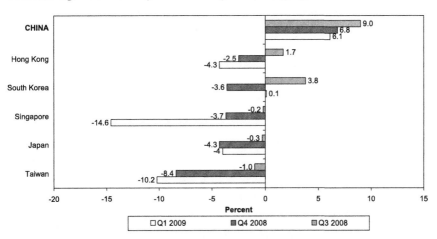

Figure 2.3.   Quarterly GDP growth of China, Japan and the NIEs, Q3 2008 to Q1 2009.
Source: EIU.

---

[6] "Chinese Premier Upbeat about China Growth, Stresses Confidence in Addressing Crisis", *Xinhua*, 29 January 2009.

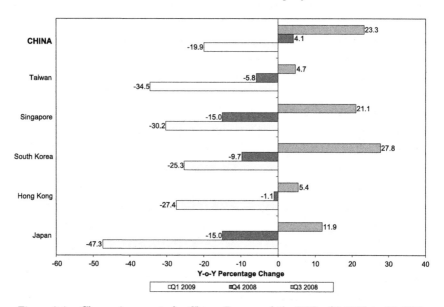

Figure 2.4.   Change in exports for China, Japan and the NIEs, Q3 2008 to Q1 2009.
Source: EIU.

and inflation growth had gone beyond the government's comfort zone. For instance, China's consumer price index was averaging nearly 8 percent from the fourth quarter of 2007 through the second quarter of 2008 (Figure 2.5).

To fight inflation and cool the overheating economy, Chinese policy makers administered policies to tighten the monetary conditions. These included raising interest rates and increasing the banks' reserve requirement ratio. From January 2006 through September 2008, China readjusted the requirement ratio upwards about 15 times. Similarly, lending rates were raised more than ten times during the same period. The central government also implemented a series of measures to slow the growth of industries and to curb overinvestment. These included tightening land supply for industrial use and taking steps to restrict the inflow of FDI. Incentives were removed from labour-intensive industries and environmental fees were slapped on polluting industries. To a certain extent, China's current economic slow-down also stemmed from a whole string of events that disrupted production in the country. These ranged from the snowstorm in early 2008 to the Sichuan earthquake in mid-2008, as well as the Olympics in August 2008.

A second explanation for the resilience of the Chinese economy is that unlike most East and Southeast Asian economies, China's economic growth is not solely driven by external demand. Rather, domestic demand,

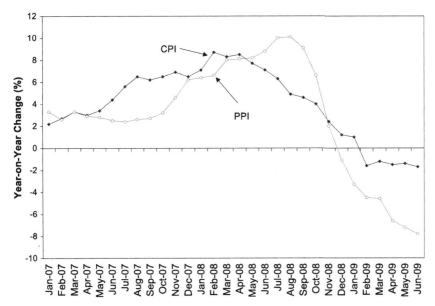

Figure 2.5. China's consumer price index and producer price index, January 2007 to June 2009.
Source: National Bureau of Statistics of China.

comprising consumption and fixed asset investment, is also a main source of growth for China. As a result, this has limited China's exposure to the current global financial crisis, which in turn allowed China to rebound from its economic slowdown faster than its neighbours, as seen in the second quarter of 2009.

China's reliance on its domestic demand for growth is not a surprise as the country is a huge continental economy with one fifth of the world's population. Furthermore, China is still in the process of industrialization and urbanization. In fact, China's urban population only amounts to about 43 percent of the country's total population. This means that there is still plenty of room for China's domestic demand to grow through infrastructure and other urban expansion projects. However, China's domestic demand is often overlooked by many Western scholars and media as they often cite the decline in China's exports as the end of its economic growth.[7]

---

[7]See "Dire Indian and Malaysian Data Fuel Asian Fears", *Financial Times*, 1 March 2009, and "China's Stimulus Challenge", *The Wall Street Journal*, 2 March 2009, for alternative views.

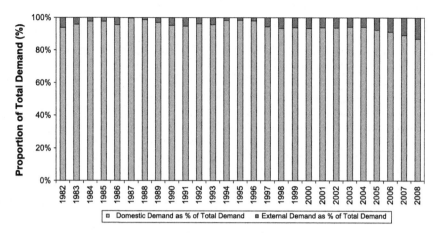

Figure 2.6.   China's sources of economic growth, 1982 to 2008.
Source: EIU.

As shown in Figure 2.6, domestic demand is the mainstay of China's total demand. From the 1980s through the 1990s, the share of domestic demand within China's total demand accounted for an average of more than 90 percent. Even after a surge in China's external trade following its accession to the World Trade Organization in 2002, domestic demand still constitutes about 85 percent of China's total demand.

A study of the fluctuation of China's past economic growth with the components of domestic demand shows that fixed investment has always been the major source of China's growth. In fact, the numerous "business cycles" (or variations in economic growth) that China experienced over the past three decades tended to swing with the ups and downs of fixed asset investment (Figure 2.7). This relationship also indicates that the central government uses fixed investment as the fiscal instrument to expand the economy when domestic deflation sets in or to curb growth when the economy faces overheating.

Indeed, the local governments' enthusiasm to develop their economies increased following Deng Xiaoping's *nanxun* in 1992, leading to a surge in domestic investment, which in turn resulted in a sharp rise in economic growth. This subsequently caused the economy to overheat. To address this, former premier Zhu Rongji cut fixed investment in the mid-1990s, allowing China's economy to achieve a "soft landing" in 1996. Fixed investment was then adjusted upwards in the late 1990s to offset the effects of the Asian financial crisis and more recently downwards to cool the economy in late 2007 and early 2008.

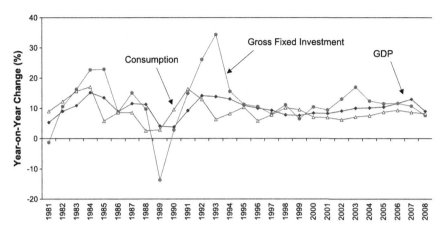

Figure 2.7.   China's domestic demand and economic growth performance, 1981 to 2008. *Source*: EIU.

The stimulus package unveiled by Beijing in November 2008 was a continuation of the central government's practice to peg China's economic growth to the level of fixed investment. In fact, the package was meticulously prepared to boost domestic demand for economic growth. The main areas of government spending include (1) public housing for low-income groups; (2) rural infrastructure such as water supply and conservation, rural roads and power grids; (3) transport infrastructure such as high-speed railways, mass transit systems, highways and airports; (4) healthcare and education; (5) ecological and environmental projects; (6) innovation and R&D, and industrial upgrading; and (7) Sichuan earthquake reconstruction (Figure 2.8).

The estimated cost for the first two years of these projects is about US$586 billion (4 trillion yuan), which is around 15 percent of China's GDP in 2007. On a global scale, China's stimulus package is the second largest in the world after the United States' US$780 billion "American Recovery and Reinvestment Plan" stimulus package which was passed in February 2009 (Figure 2.9). It is, however, the largest among the stimulus packages unveiled by Asian and European economies.

China's ability to unveil such a massive stimulus package is largely attributed to its strong fiscal record. First, China's budget deficit has been decreasing rapidly in recent years. From 2000 to the end of 2007, China's fiscal balance increased from a deficit of nearly 3 percent of GDP to a surplus of 0.7 percent of GDP. On the other hand, most developed economies, particularly the United States, have been experiencing a growing

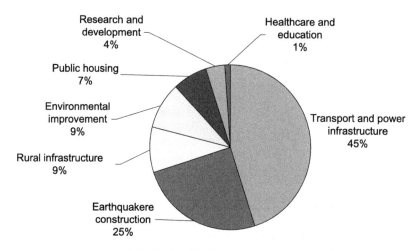

Total value:4 trillion yuan (US$586 billion)

Figure 2.8.   Areas of spending in China's stimulus package (%).
Source: National Development and Reform Commission.

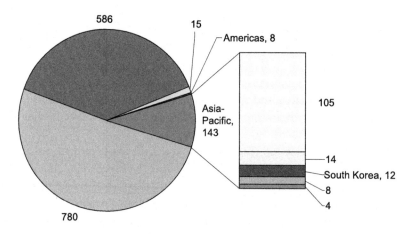

Figure 2.9.   Economic stimulus packages worldwide (US$ billion).
Source: Asian Wall Street Journal.

budget deficit and rising public debt. For instance, the United States'
budget balance dropped from a surplus of 2.4 percent of GDP in 2000
to a deficit of 3.2 percent of GDP by the end of 2008 (Figure 2.10). Because
of the massive fiscal stimulus package, China's budget deficit was posed to
increase quite significantly in 2009. In March 2009, Premier Wen Jiabao

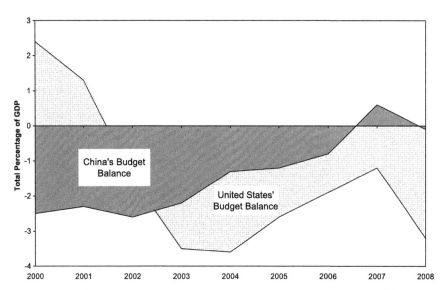

Figure 2.10.   China's and the United States' budget balance, 2000 to 2009 (% of total GDP).
Source: EIU.

projected China's fiscal deficit budget to hit 950 billion yuan (US$139 billion), which would be the highest in six decades. Despite the deficit surge, China's constant deficit drops in previous years provided room for issuing more bonds in 2009.[8]

In addition, China's public debt is declining. This allows Beijing to flex its fiscal muscle to fight the recession. From 2003 to 2007, China's public debt decreased from nearly 30 percent of GDP to only about 18 percent of GDP. In comparison, the United States' public debt increased from 35 percent of total GDP to nearly 40 percent of GDP during the same period (Figure 2.11).

Besides, China's savings rate is very high. On average, a Chinese household saves about 26 percent of total disposable income. This is considerably higher than the savings rate of most developed economies (Figure 2.12). For instance, the United States' savings rate was less than 0.5 percent of total disposable income in 2007.[9]

---

[8] "China Budgets $139b Fiscal Deficit in Crisis Fight", *China Daily*, 5 March 2009.
[9] "Consumers Are Saving More and Spending Less", *The New York Times*, 2 February 2009.

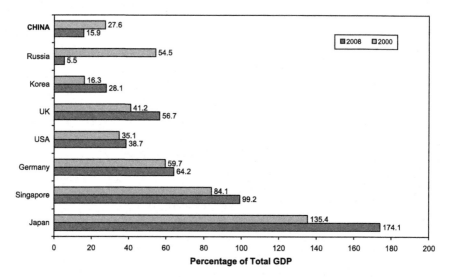

Figure 2.11.   China's public debt compared to other countries, 2000 and 2008.
Source: EIU.

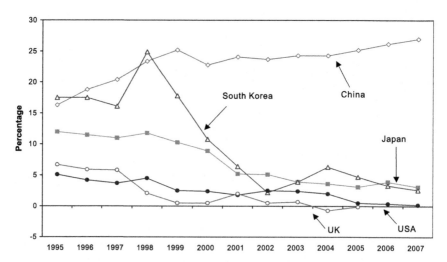

Figure 2.12.   Household savings rate in China and selected economies, 1995 to 2007.
Source: China Bureau of Statistics; OECD.

China's banks are also well capitalized. In fact, three of the world's top ten cash-rich companies are Chinese banks (Table 2.1). Furthermore, the three Chinese banks in the list, namely Bank of China, Industrial and Commercial Bank of China (ICBC) and China Construction Bank, have a

Table 2.1.   Top ten cash-rich companies as at end of 2008.

	Companies	Net Cash (US$ billion)
1	Berkshire Hathaway	106
2	**Bank of China**	**101**
3	**ICBC**	**89**
4	**China Construction Bank**	**82**
5	ExxonMobil	28
6	China Mobile	26
7	Apple	25
8	Cisco Systems	20
9	Microsoft	19
10	Google	14
	TOTAL NET CASH	**540**

Source: Bloomberg.

total net cash of US$272 billion, which is nearly 55 percent of the total net cash of all the top ten companies.

Although Beijing's response to the global downturn is focused on boosting domestic demand, this does not mean that it is disregarding its external trade. In fact, Premier Wen urged major economies to continue to maintain a liberalized trading environment and made it clear that Beijing was against taking on any protectionist measures. The Chinese premier also admitted that China would not be able to fully recover from the current global recession if global demand remained weak. In all, it shows that China still views external demand as playing a key supporting role in inducing growth of the economy.

In addition, although China's external demand constitutes only a small share of its GDP growth, it has been rising in recent years, especially after China's accession to the World Trade Organization in 2002. As Figure 2.13 illustrates, the share of the contribution of net exports to China's GDP growth had been growing for the past decade from about 6 percent in 1998 to over 11 percent by the end of 2008. This rising trend indicates that external demand is set to play a more important supporting role in China's economic growth in the future.

In particular, industries in Guangdong's Pearl River Delta, China's manufacturing and export hub, and other coastal areas are highly dependent on external demand. Therefore, it is crucial for the external situation to improve before these regions can recover from the effects of the global financial crisis. These regions of mostly foreign-funded firms were badly hit

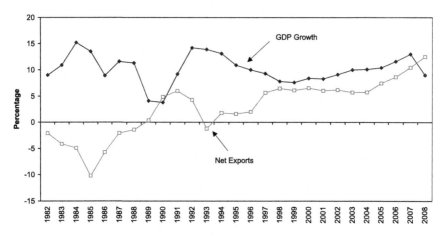

Figure 2.13.   Contribution of China's net exports to GDP, 1982 to 2008.
Source: EIU.

by the crisis. In fact, Huang Yunlong, vice governor of Guangdong province, called 2008 "the most difficult year after the 1998 Asian financial crisis". Huang's remark was not an understatement. According to the Guangdong Statistics Bureau, 100,600 new firms were established in 2008, but by the end of the year, more than 62,400 had been eliminated. This alarming closure rate has also resulted in massive job losses. In fact, the Statistics Bureau reported that an estimated 600,000 migrants lost their jobs in 2008.[10]

For this financial crisis, however, the Chinese leadership is more concerned with stimulating domestic demand than external demand, as it is aware that the weakening global demand is beyond the control of the Chinese government. Nonetheless, it is important to note that most of the measures taken to stimulate the domestic market, such as the stimulus projects, are also aimed at creating jobs.

Loosening Monetary Policies

To fight the recession and to ensure the effectiveness of the massive stimulus package, Beijing also made important adjustments to loosen its monetary conditions. Some of these measures include cutting interest rates and

---

[10] "600,000 Migrant Workers Leave Guangdong amid Financial Crisis", *Xinhua*, 9 January 2009.

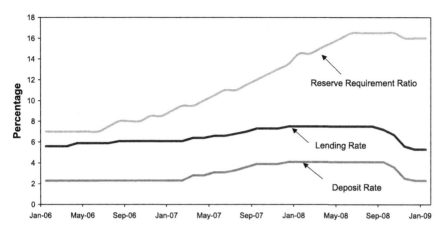

Figure 2.14. China's lending rate, deposit rate and bank reserve requirement ratio, January 2006 to January 2009.
Source: EIU.

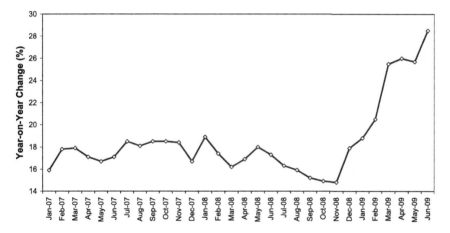

Figure 2.15. China's money supply (M2) growth, January 2007 to June 2009 (%).
Source: EIU.

lifting lending limits on commercial banks. As Figure 2.14 shows, China's central bank had adjusted lending rates quite significantly downwards from 7.2 percent to 5.6 percent between August 2008 and November 2008. The lending rate was further revised to 5.3 percent in December 2008. Similarly, the central bank cut half a percentage point from the reserve requirement ratio for banks, from an all-time high of 16.5 percent to 16 percent in December 2008.

As part of the blueprint to ease the country's monetary conditions, the central bank has also started to increase China's money supply. As shown in Figure 2.15, China's money supply in December 2008 and January 2009 had registered its highest year-on-year percentage change since May 2008, of 17.9 percent and 18.8 percent respectively. This continued well into 2009, reaching 20.5 percent, 25.5 percent and 26 percent in February, March and April respectively. According to the State Council, China would continue to maintain a high level of money supply growth of around 17 percent in 2009.

With the stabilization of the country's runaway inflation in the second half of 2008, the central government would be able to continue relaxing the country's monetary conditions in 2009. The massive foreign reserves and favourable trade surplus also allowed China to maintain the stability of its currency, both important monetary factors for China to maintain the competitiveness of its economy and its attractiveness to FDI inflow.

Early Signs of Recovery and the Road Ahead

The policies undertaken by Beijing to boost the economy were effective in boosting the Chinese economy. Other than allowing China to post a growth of 7.9 percent in the second quarter of 2009, it also helped improve the domestic economic environment. First, China's purchasing management index (PMI), which measures new orders made by the manufacturing sector, registered an increase, has stopped its slide and has maintained a level of over 50 percent since March 2009 (Figure 2.16).

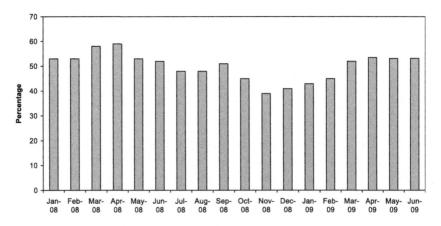

Figure 2.16.   China's purchasing management index, January 2008 to June 2009.
Source: RCIF.

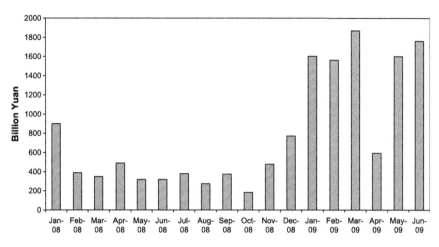

Figure 2.17. Bank loans made in China, January 2008 to June 2009.
Source: People's Bank of China.

Second, China's credit problem seems to be easing. For instance, bank loans made in China in January 2009 rocketed to 1.62 trillion yuan (US$237 billion), reversing months of decline in bank loans (Figure 2.17). Since then (except in April 2009), loans made by Chinese banks were averaging above 1.5 trillion yuan. The massive growth in bank loans signals that banks are lining up to provide funds to developers for the stimulus package projects. This could be a blessing for cash-strapped domestic enterprises trying to stay afloat amid shrinking overseas demand and waning consumer confidence.

Overall, these are definitely indications that the Chinese economy is reacting positively to the central government's measures. This should place China firmly in pole position to recover from the current global downturn once the global economic conditions stabilize. However, as soon as China's recovery gains momentum, it is important for Beijing to introduce measures to reverse the effects of the emergency actions taken to free credit markets and boost demand.

As the world is beginning to witness, the emergency actions taken by economies around the world, particularly the United States, to free credit markets and boost demand are likely to bring a second round of inflation.[11] In fact, signs of inflationary pressure could be seen with the recent spike

---

[11] "The Biggest Bill in History", *The Economist*, 13 June 2009.

of oil prices from about US$40 per barrel in March 2009 to over US$70 per barrel by mid-June 2009 as well as the 20 percent increase in raw material prices and the surge in gold futures to over US$1,000 during the same period. Furthermore, signs of a weakening dollar could already be seen with yields of the ten-year Treasury bill jumping from around 2 percent at the end of 2008 to almost 4 percent by early June 2009.[12]

In order to cushion itself from the imminent round of inflation, China has to prepare to tighten its loose monetary policy by increasing interest rates and reducing the money supply once China's economy stabilizes. This, however, has to be done through a coordinated effort with other economies so as not to derail the recovery process of the global economy. The central government should also reduce government spending in order to maintain a sizeable deficit, thereby keeping the country's fiscal position in check and mitigating the cost to the people.

Along with these short-term responses, China also has to make long-term adjustments to its economy. For instance, it has to step up efforts to liberalize its financial and capital markets. So far, Beijing seems to be aware of this developing trend with its announcement of internationalizing the Chinese currency and turning Shanghai into an international financial centre.[13] China is also showing more willingness to take on a bigger leadership role in the post-recession global economy. For instance, Beijing has become a leading voice in supporting calls for less dependency on the US dollar. In recent months, it has suggested the establishment of a super-sovereign reserve currency and has been spearheading efforts with BRICS (Brazil, Russia, India and China) countries in purchasing IMF instead of US Treasury bonds.[14] Besides, China has concluded a number of currency swap agreements with its trading partners and is exploring the idea of conducting bilateral trade using the Chinese yuan and the respective trading partner's currency.[15] All in all, these developing events are clear indications that the world economy may progress into a new system where China will have a more important role to play.

More important, as it is almost certain that the global economy will take on a different shape once the recession is over, China has to reassess its growth strategy. One way is to shift its engine of growth from exports

---

[12] "This Way Out", *The Economist*, 6 June 2009.
[13] Lan Xinzhen, "Rebranding Shanghai", *Beijing Review*, 14 May 2009.
[14] "BRICS Building Road to Global Economic Recovery", *China Daily*, 18 June 2009.
[15] "Malaysia, China Consider Ending Trade in Dollars", *The Wall Street Journal*, 4 June 2009.

to domestic demand. As shown earlier, because of the strength of China's domestic demand, the country has been able to shield itself from the full impact of the global financial crisis. By spending on building infrastructure such as railways, roads and power grids, China has been able to prop up demand, thus allowing the economy to rebound faster and more strongly than its East Asian neighbours. However, relying on fixed investment is only effective in the short term. In order to ensure that domestic demand will remain a sustainable source of growth for the Chinese economy in the long term, China has to increase the share of consumption, particularly private consumption, in domestic demand.

To encourage Chinese households to spend more and save less will be a challenging task, especially since the share of private consumption in China's GDP has been decreasing in recent years. From 1995 to 2008, the ratio of consumption to China's GDP fell from about 45 percent to around 35 percent. This took place against the backdrop of an increase in household savings. To improve private consumption, Beijing could enlarge the country's social safety net. This can be achieved through the provision of cheaper healthcare and education as well as the establishment of an adequate pension system and a more developed financial system that makes borrowing easier. The consumption behaviour of Chinese households can also be changed by expanding their household income through wage increase or by restructuring the economy to be more knowledge-driven and value-added rather than labour-intensive. In addition, China could also allow its exchange rate to rise. This would lift consumers' real purchasing power.[16] How effectively China can address the issue of increasing private consumption in the post-financial crisis period remains to be seen, but it is definite that the destructive effect of the crisis has catalyzed the process.

A Closer Look at Consumption

There has been a chorus of calls both outside and inside China for measures to stimulate consumption in China. Arguments have been advanced based on the Japanese experience. From the 神武景気 (1954–1957) to 岩戸景気 (1959–1961), Japan's growth was driven by both internal consumption and exports.[17]

---

[16] "The Spend is Nigh", *The Economist*, 30 June 2009.
[17] 时寒冰, 中国怎麽办－当次货危及改变世界 (北京: 机械工业出版社, 2008). (Shi Hanbing, *What Must China Do? The World Changed by the Current Currency Crisis* (Beijing: China Machine Press, 2008).)

Apart from the Japanese experience, there are a few good reasons for such calls in China. First, it would redress the trade imbalance between China and the West. Second, it would improve the general living standards of the Chinese people. Third, it would provide a huge demand pull which acts as a driver of economic growth both for China and its trading partners. However, for consumption to play a positive role in economic development, especially in the long term, certain conditions are needed. For one thing, the nature of the consumption is important. It can be productive like building a school, or wasteful like overconsumption of food. When carried out properly, consumption can boost productivity, as users of washing machines can easily testify.

Though a government cannot dictate the details of household consumption, it can use taxation and subsidy to steer patterns of consumption. It can impose taxes on goods like liquor and cigarettes and provide subsidies for the installation of solar panels and other kinds of green technologies. At the same time, the government needs to do more to ensure the quality of products and services. The case of adulterated milk has certainly not increased the confidence of Chinese consumers. Moreover, by making international headlines, such cases have done great damage to China's international image and called into question the safety and quality of Chinese engineering projects abroad.[18] Regarding issues of such nature, the government would do well to encourage the roles of strong and independent consumer bodies, and engage them actively and positively in order to guarantee the quality and integrity of products and services. This may well turn out to be one of the happy unintended consequences of the financial crisis.

---

[18]David Barboza, "A San Francisco Bridge, Made in China", *International Herald Tribune*, 27 June 2011.

Chapter Three

Shanghai as an International Financial Centre

In March 2009, China's State Council announced an ambitious plan to transform Shanghai into a major international financial centre, on par with Hong Kong, Singapore, New York and London by 2020.

The State Council's announcement was timely as it came at a time when, in the wake of the 2008–2009 financial crisis, China was assuming a leading role in global economic affairs. Indeed, China was set to replace Japan as the second largest economy in the world in early 2009. It is also the world's largest manufacturing base and the biggest commodity importer. Besides, China holds 40 percent (or around US$2 trillion) of the world's foreign exchange reserves and is also the world's largest holder of US Treasury bills.

In addition, the country has the world's top three banks in terms of market capitalization (see Table A.1 in Appendix). In 2009, China (including Macau) accounted for 47.8 percent of the total value of IPOs worldwide (that of the USA was 14.6 percent) — another indication of the growing importance of the Chinese financial market.[1] More importantly, China is becoming bolder in the internationalization of its currency and is actively exploring means to reduce its dependency on the US dollar.

The emergency actions taken by various countries, particularly those of the United States, to free credit markets and boost demand are likely to cause inflation.[2] In fact, signs of inflationary pressure could be seen in the spike of oil prices from about US$40 per barrel in March 2009 to over US$60 per barrel by the end of June 2009, as well as the 20 percent increase in raw material prices and the surge in gold futures to over US$1,000 during the same period.

Inflation is no good news for the US dollar. Signs of a weakening dollar can already be seen in the yields of the ten-year Treasury bill jumping from around 2 percent at the end of 2008 to almost 4 percent by early June

---

[1] "Equity Firms Target CICC", *The Wall Street Journal*, 23 February 2010, pp. 1, 16.
[2] "The Biggest Bill in History", *The Economist*, 13 June 2009.

2009.[3] As the global economy shows signs of life, there will be even more downward pressure on the US dollar as investors become less risk averse and do not need the dollar's security.

With this developing trend, China is keen to avoid the "US dollar trap". Coined by Nobel laureate Paul Krugman in his *New York Times* article, the term refers to the massive value loss in foreign reserves due to a depreciated US dollar.[4]

Beijing has come up with a number of ways to address the dollar trap. In March 2009, Zhou Xiaochuan, governor of the People's Bank of China, called for the establishment of a super-sovereign reserve currency based on existing special drawing rights to replace the US dollar.[5] Furthermore, since December 2008, Beijing has concluded a series of currency swap agreements with its trading partners and has been experimenting with the idea of conducting trade and investment activities using the yuan and the respective partner's currency. To date, the People's Bank of China has arranged six bilateral currency swaps, totalling more than 650 billion yuan (US$95 billion), with countries including Japan, South Korea, Malaysia, Hong Kong, Brazil and Argentina.[6]

Currency swaps could be used for trade settlements between China and its trading partners. As a start, Shanghai, Shenzhen, Zhuhai, Dongguang and Nanning were chosen by the Chinese government to use the renminbi for trade settlements. The first currency swap agreement between China and Hong Kong, which involved more than 440 companies, took effect in June 2009.[7] The Chinese government is also planning to include the purchase of renminbi financial products in the currency swap agreements.

Shanghai as an International Financial Centre

The State Council's announcement is significant as it marked for the first time a concrete national-level backing and recognition of Shanghai's status as a global financial hub. Prior to that, it was only functioning as China's

---

[3] "This Way Out", *The Economist*, 6 June 2009.

[4] Paul Krugman, "China's Dollar Trap", *The New York Times*, 2 April 2009, http://www.nytimes.com/2009/04/03/opinion/03krugman.html [accessed 1 June 2009].

[5] Yang Mu and Chen Shaofeng, "Can China Reduce Foreign Reserve Risks?", *China Daily*, 20 May 2009.

[6] "BIS-China, Brazil Working on Trade FX Deal — Cenbanks", *Reuters*, 28 June 2009.

[7] "Deal signed on Yuan settlement; Chinese currency may be used for cross-border Trade from next month," *South China Morning Post*, 30 June 2009.

de facto financial hub and has recently been jostling for this position with Beijing. According to Liu Tienan, Vice Minister of the National Development and Reform Commission (NDRC), the State Council gave its official blessing to Shanghai simply because the city was the "most qualified metropolitan city on the Chinese mainland to pursue the ambition".

As stated in the guidelines of the State Council's decision, the process to build Shanghai into an international financial hub encompasses features such as using the yuan for international trade settlement, developing private equity and developing a reinsurance market, and encouraging overseas enterprises to issue yuan-denominated bonds in China (Table 3.1).

The Chinese authorities need to introduce a more transparent and independent legal system and promulgate favourable tax policies to attract financial companies. The State Council also has asked the city to step up efforts to shore up its soft infrastructure. These include incentives and measures to attract and train financial talents. Banks in China are urged to provide sophisticated investment products.

Historically, Shanghai has been a centre for trade and commerce, especially after its establishment as a treaty port in the mid-19th century. By the 1920s and 1930s, the city had flourished to become one of the world's major cities and an important entrepôt. Consequently, this led to

Table 3.1. Key measures to support Shanghai's development as a financial hub.

Key Measures
1 Conduct trade settlement in yuan on a trial basis
2 Fully tap the financial market in Shanghai in terms of clearing in yuan
3 Develop over-the-counter (OTC) markets for non-listed companies in the Yangtze River Delta
4 Formulate a mechanism to help companies trading on the OTC markets to be transferred to the main stock boards
5 Develop pension products that offer tax breaks, to encourage people to pay into pensions
6 Encourage more international development institutions to issue yuan-denominated bonds
7 Study plans to allow overseas enterprises to issue yuan-denominated bonds in China
8 Allow qualified overseas companies to issue yuan-denominated shares
9 Step up development of the reinsurance market
10 Give priority in terms of business expansion to securities and fund-management joint ventures
11 Encourage financial institutions to cover a wider range of businesses
12 Encourage the development of private equity and venture capital companies

Source: China Daily.

the growth of Shanghai's financial sector. However, the city's progress as an economic and financial hub was interrupted by political events and it was overshadowed by Hong Kong after 1949.

Since China's open-door policy in 1978, Shanghai has been striving to regain its status as the premier economic and financial hub of China. This process was consolidated and gathered speed following the Pudong New Area Project initiated by Deng Xiaoping after his *nanxun* in 1992. Thereafter, Shanghai has experienced spectacular economic growth lasting until now. As Figure 3.1 shows, Shanghai's GDP has been growing at a double-digit rate for most years since 1992.

Shanghai's revival also took a different course from that of most Chinese cities. Instead of focusing on the growth of the manufacturing sector, as seen in cities such as Shenzhen, Tianjin and Beijing, Shanghai's economy was powered by the service sector. As seen in Figure 3.2, Shanghai's service sector contributed nearly 54 percent of the city's GDP in 2008. It also absorbed about 54 percent of the city's labour force in the same year.

In this sense, Shanghai has a relatively complete financial sector. In 2008, Shanghai's financial industry generated an added value of about 144 billion yuan (US$21 billion). This is an increase of about 15 percent from the previous year and about 10 percent of Shanghai's total GDP in 2008 (Figure 3.3). By the end of 2008, there were a total of 689 financial institutions in the city. Of that, 124 were commercial banks, 291 were

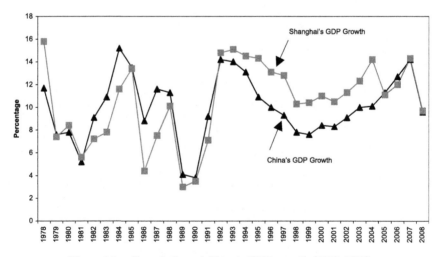

Figure 3.1.   Shanghai's and China's GDP growth (1978–2008).
Source: Shanghai Statistical Yearbook 2009.

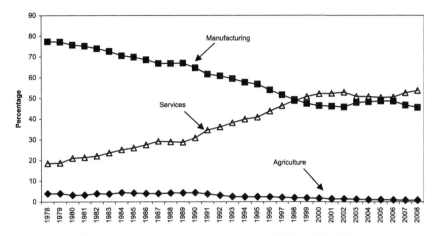

Figure 3.2.   Components of Shanghai's GDP (1978–2008).
Source: Shanghai Statistical Yearbook (various issues).

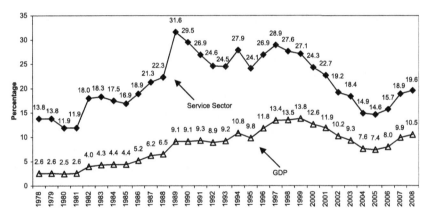

Figure 3.3.   Percentage share of financial sector in Shanghai's total GDP and service sector (1978–2008).
Source: Shanghai Statistical Yearbook (various issues).

insurance companies and 94 securities companies. Of the total, 165 were foreign banks.[8]

Shanghai is also home to the Shanghai Stock Exchange (SSE). As at the end of 2007, the SSE had 860 listed companies with a combined capitalization of US$3.7 trillion. This made the SSE the world's sixth largest stock exchange in terms of market capitalization.

---

[8]Lan Xinzhen, "Rebranding Shanghai", *Beijing Review*, 14 May 2009.

Table 3.2.   Financial institutions in Shanghai since 1990.

Institutions	Function	Founding Year	Status or Scale
Shanghai Stock Exchange	Main, capital market (equity, bonds)	1990	80 percent of total trading turnover in China
Foreign exchange trading centre	Foreign exchange	1994	Head office of national trading market
Interbank loan centre	Money market	1996	National centre for interbank trading
RMB bond trading centre	Money market	1997	National centre for bond trading
Shanghai Futures Exchange	Rubber, copper, aluminium and fuel oil	1999	60 percent of futures trading volume in China
Shanghai Gold Exchange	Gold market	2002	The only gold market
Note market service centre	Provides note transaction information and service	2003	Principal note pricing system in China
Shanghai Petroleum Exchange	Futures transactions	2006	The only petroleum market in China
China Financial Futures Exchange	Financial derivatives transactions	2006	The only derivatives market in China

Source: Soogil Young *et al.* (eds.), *Competition Among Financial Centres in Asia-Pacific: Prospects, Benefits, Risks and Policy Changes* (ISEAS: Singapore, 2009), p. 234.

Since it was set up in 1990, trading within the SSE has gradually been liberalized to allow the inflow of foreign funds and yuan-denominated trading. For instance, the SSE introduced the Qualified Foreign Institutional Investor (QFII) programme in 2003 and the Qualified Domestic Institutional Investor (QDII) programme in 2006.[9] The QFII allowed foreign investors to buy yuan-denominated shares in the SSE, while the QDII allowed domestic financial institutions to invest in shares in offshore markets. These measures are seen as milestones because China's capital market had always been heavily regulated by the central government since it adopted the open-door policy.

In addition to the stock exchange, Shanghai has introduced a number of financial institutions since 1990. These include a foreign exchange market, RMB bond trading centre, gold exchange, futures exchange for commodities and derivatives market (see Table 3.2).

---

[9]See Lu Ding and Li Ning, "China's Capital Market Reform: Problems and Prospects", in John Wong and Liu Wei (eds.), *China's Surging Economy: Adjusting for More Balanced Development* (Singapore: World Scientific, 2007), pp. 282–283, for more details on reforms carried out in the Shanghai Stock Exchange.

Challenges Ahead

Shanghai has to overcome a number of hurdles before it can become a full-fledged international financial centre. First are the issues of non-convertibility of the Chinese yuan and the ban on capital flows. All major international financial centres do not face these issues, which puts Shanghai at a disadvantage. As the two issues come under the jurisdiction of the central government, there is nothing Shanghai can do about them.

The non-convertibility of the yuan is part of the macroeconomic policy of promoting exports as a means of generating economic growth and creating employment. Beijing's policies strongly suggest that the finance sector must serve the economy, which means that financial policies must be subsumed under economic policies. The prospects for currency convertibility are good if China continues to upgrade its economy to higher-value-adding activities and solve its unemployment problem. Judging from past government behaviour, Beijing is likely to adopt a gradualist approach and to do so on its own terms.

As part of this gradualist approach, the government is using currency swaps to settle trade between China and some of its trading partners. This is a win-win situation for both China and its major trading partners, though on balance it benefits China more. The arrangement is halfway to the final stage of a floating exchange rate for the yuan. As China is moving in this direction, it is also relaxing its control on capital flows.

China is very cautious about capital control for good reasons. In the 1997 Asian financial crisis, free currency flows allowed currency speculators to wreak havoc in Hong Kong, South Korea and the ASEAN countries.[10] This caution has been further buttressed by the 2008 financial crisis. Both China and India, with their control of capital flows, need not worry about the danger of a currency crisis. A number of eminent pro-market economists have strongly argued for control of short-term speculative capital flows.[11] Even the International Monetary Fund, which has a history of advocating free capital flows, has modified its position.[12]

Capital control consists of a range of measures targeted at different types of capital flow. In fact, China does not impose a blanket ban on capital flows. Since its economic reform, China has welcomed manufacturing FDI

---

[10]Paul Krugman, *The Return of Depression Economics and the Crisis of 2008* (New York: W. W. Norton, 2009).
[11]Michael Lim Mah Hui and Lim Chin, *The Great Financial Crisis and Challenges for Asia* (Singapore: ISEAS, 2010).
[12]"Fundamental Questions", *The Economist*, 20 February 2010.

and allowed repatriation of legitimate profits. It also allows remittance of funds for overseas study as well as for corporate investment and trade. Chinese tourists going abroad and foreign tourists entering China are allowed to bring with them a reasonable amount of money.

In June 2009, China approved the listing of foreign companies on the SSE.[13] This was an unprecedented move and a huge step forward in liberalizing China's capital market as the policy would not only set the stage for the inflow of more foreign funds, but also allow foreign companies to raise capital in China. Shanghai also permits locally incorporated foreign banks to issue yuan-denominated bonds and allows China-based foreign companies to be listed on the SSE. These are signs that the government is gradually liberalizing its financial market.

Secondly, Shanghai has to strengthen its position vis-à-vis Beijing, which enjoys comparable financial prowess. In 2007, Beijing's financial sector was worth 112.7 billion yuan (US$16.1 billion), making up about 12.5 percent of the city's GDP, while that of Shanghai was worth around 119.6 billion yuan (US$17.1 billion), or about 10 percent of its GDP.[14] In addition, Beijing is home to 677 financial institutions and most of the headquarters of China's national and foreign banks. In 2007, the savings-to-GDP ratio in Shanghai was 249 percent, and the loan-to-GDP ratio was 178 percent. These figures are much higher than the national average (156 percent and 105 percent), but they are only about half of Beijing's (429 percent and 230 percent).[15]

Beijing's strength is based on the fact that the Chinese government still plays a very important role in the economy. Government investment is the most important driving force for China's economy, the main source of bank deposits and the largest loan issuer. In addition, IPOs and the reissuing of shares are controlled by the China Securities Regulatory Commission in Beijing. As a result, most of China's national and foreign banks as well as the MNCs and local enterprises prefer to locate their headquarters there. However, unlike Shanghai, Beijing does not have an institutionalized stock market, money market, currency market and futures market. Its financial infrastructure is less established.

---

[13] "Shanghai Stock Market Opens to Foreign Firms", *Telegraph*, 1 May 2009.

[14] "Beijing's Financial Dream", *Beijing Review*, 24 May 2008.

[15] Shahid Yusuf and Kaoru Nabeshima, *Two Dragon Heads: Contrasting Development Paths for Beijing and Shanghai* (Washington: World Bank, 2010), pp. 89–94.

Given the nature of the political system and interest group lobbying, it will not be easy for Shanghai to gain mileage over Beijing. However, Shanghai hosts the country's leading stock market, is more commercially oriented and has a vast industrial base in the Yangtze River Delta and an economically dynamic hinterland. The deepening of the marketization of the Chinese economy is likely to weaken the role of Beijing as a financial centre relative to Shanghai. In most of the big countries (such as the USA, Germany, Brazil and India), the financial centre is not the political centre.

Thirdly, China can allow more financial products to be made available to investors, e.g. futures markets and markets for bonds, derivatives and currency trade. At the same time, an international financial centre needs to have effective supervision and regulation. The importance of this point has been amply demonstrated by the 2008 financial crisis. These activities require a million well-trained and experienced finance professionals, especially those in senior positions.[16]

Shanghai has responded to this shortage in human resources with a two-pronged approach. It has sent a number of delegations to New York, Hong Kong and Singapore to recruit highly qualified professionals, a task made easier by the large numbers of them being laid off during the financial crisis. The city has also allocated 320 million yuan to set up Shanghai Advanced Institute of Finance (上海高级金融学院) at Jiaotong University (ranked fourth in China), with the aim of turning it into a world-class research and teaching institute. The institute has an educational exchange programme with the National University of Singapore Business School. Moreover, Shanghai has Fudan University (ranked third in China) and Shanghai University of Finance and Economics (上海财经大学).

Fourthly, Shanghai still has a lot to do to bring its current financial infrastructure up to international standards. China has to improve its accounting standards, legal framework for business, corporate governance and other soft infrastructure. As an indication of the inadequate legal framework, international banks usually bring cross-border transactions initiated in Shanghai to Hong Kong or Singapore in order to execute them there, with the contracts governed by Anglo-Saxon legal terms.[17]

---

[16] "Shanghai Finance Lacks 1 Million Professionals; Government Invests 3 Million to Build Finance Institute", *Xinhua*, 4 May 2009, http://news.xinhuanet.com/fortune/2009-05/04/content_11306348.htm.

[17] Xu Mingqi, "Building the Shanghai International Financial Centre: Strategic Targets, Challenges and Opportunities", in Soogil Young *et al.* (eds.), *Competition Among Financial Centres in Asia-Pacific* (Singapore: ISEAS, 2009).

Table 3.3.   The global financial centres index: 2009 and 2010 rankings.

Financial Centre	GFCI 2010 Ranking	GFCI 2009 Ranking
London	1	1
New York	2	2
Hong Kong	3	3
Singapore	4	4
Tokyo	5	7
Chicago	6	8
Zurich	7	6
Geneva	8	9
Shenzhen	9	5
Sydney	10	11
Shanghai	**11**	**10**
Toronto	12	13
Frankfurt	13	12
Boston	14	17
Beijing	**15**	**23**
Taipei	21	25

Source: The Global Financial Centres Index 5.

According to the latest Global Financial Centres Index (GFCI), which ranks the competitiveness of global financial centres, Shanghai was ranked 11th out of a total of 75 centres in 2010, one place down from its 10th position in the previous year (Table 3.3). The financial cities that Shanghai wants to emulate, namely London, New York, Hong Kong and Singapore, were in the top four.[18]

As one of the world's leading financial centres, Hong Kong is able to provide invaluable insights for Shanghai, especially in areas such as liberalizing its capital market. Hong Kong could also help Shanghai improve its corporate and commercial infrastructure, such as its corporate governance and business legal system (see Table A.2 in the Appendix for a SWOT analysis of Hong Kong and Shanghai as international financial centres).

Contrary to the buzz that Hong Kong could become a has-been,[19] Hong Kong is emerging as a viable alternative to New York and London, particularly for large companies in emerging markets which do not have easy access to mainland China. Hong Kong led a consortium consisting of the Shanghai Stock Exchange and Shenzhen Stock Exchange to raise a

---

[18] "London and New York lead world in latest global financial centres report," CPI Financial, 14 March 2010.
[19] "Shanghai surprise" *Newsweek*, 15 June 2009.

combined US$52 billion in IPO proceeds in 2009. That is much more than the US$27 billion raised at the NYSE and Nasdaq, and the US$2 billion in London.[20] While Shanghai is on its bumpy journey to fulfil its ambition, Hong Kong will continue to function as the main international financial centre for China.

Appendix

Table A.1.   Top ten biggest banks in 2004 and 2009.

	2004 Ranking		2008 Ranking	
Ranking	Banks	Market Value (US$ Billion)	Banks	Market Value (US$ Billion)
1	Citigroup	259	Industrial and Commercial Bank of China	252
2	HSBC	163	China Construction Bank	180
3	Bank of America	118	Bank of China	151
4	Wells Fargo	97	HSBC	140
5	RBS	89	JP Morgan Chase	125
6	UBS	86	Wells Fargo	110
7	JP Morgan Chase	85	Banco Santander	95
8	Mitsubishi Tokyo	63	Bank of America	85
9	Wachovia	61	Mitsubishi UFJ Financial	75
10	Bank One	60	BNP Paribas	74

Source: Soogil Young *et al.* (eds.), *Competition Among Financial Centres in Asia-Pacific: Prospects, Benefits, Risks and Policy Changes* (ISEAS: Singapore, 2009), p. xlvii.

Table A.2.   SWOT analysis of Hong Kong and Shanghai as international financial centres.

Hong Kong	Shanghai
Strengths	**Strengths**
o High level of transparency of the government and its policies	o Very large economic power and abundant human resources
o Political and social stability	o Large domestic capital market
o Equitable treatment of foreigners	o Very good potential for continuation of high growth
o Foreign exchange stability and abundant liquidity	o Possesses a large amount of domestic savings
o Superb financial infrastructure	
o Minimal interference by financial supervisory/regulatory authority	

(*Continued*)

---

[20] "Taking Stock of Hong Kong", *The Wall Street Journal*, 5–7 February 2010.

Table A.2.   (*Continued*)

Hong Kong	Shanghai
Strengths	**Strengths**
o Predictable legal environment	
o Workforce with good financial expertise and international experience	
o English-speaking population	
o Regional headquarters for many global financial institutions, including investment banks	
Weaknesses	**Weaknesses**
o Limited local market size	o Regulations hindering efficient functioning of the market mechanism
o Serious air pollution	o Limited openness to foreign investment
	o Slow internationalization of the capital markets
	o Soft financial infrastructure development lagging behind hard infrastructure development
	o Limited command of the English language among the local population
Opportunities	**Opportunities**
o Physical proximity with China	o Opening of the market to foreign firms and investors
o A bridge connecting foreign companies to investors in China	
Threats	**Threats**
o Competition with Shanghai as a financial centre	o Competition with Hong Kong to become the main financial centre in China

Source: Soogil Young *et al.* (eds.), *Competition Among Financial Centres in Asia-Pacific: Prospects, Benefits, Risks and Policy Changes* (ISEAS: Singapore, 2009), pp. 7 and 15.

Chapter Four

The Renminbi Debate

The year 2010 may be seen as a year of unhappy economic relationships between China and the USA, with each side accusing the other of pursuing economic policies that run contrary to accepted international rules.[1] The USA and Europe claimed that China had been deliberately maintaining a cheap Chinese currency as a means of boosting its exports, to the detriment of their trade balance with China. With deep interdependencies between the two countries, a cheap yuan benefits certain sectors in both countries, just as a revalued currency would benefit other groups in the two countries.

A key problem is America's huge trade deficit with China. It can be reduced if US companies sell what Chinese companies wish to buy. But Washington restricts such sales. A way out is for Chinese firms to buy European technologies and assets. With the money, European companies can buy American technologies and assets. This will reduce global imbalances and the dollar will recover, providing a benign environment for growth in the real economy. Closer ties between Asia and Europe can also operate as a restraint and counsel to reduce American unilateralism.

Gradual Rise of the Yuan

At the heart of the thorny economic relationship between China and the USA are the American trade deficit and the huge buildup of foreign reserves held by China in US dollars. To put it simply, it is the result of America spending too much and saving too little and running up debts. Though the solution is clear-cut, namely save more and spend less, it is not easy to implement. With this as the backdrop, there have been incessant calls by Washington for China to revalue its yuan upwards. The idea behind it is that such a move will reduce the US trade deficit.

Whether as a response to US pressure or otherwise, the People's Bank of China announced on 19 June 2010 that it would end a two-year peg of

---

[1] Zbigniew Brzezinski, "How to Stay Friends With China", *New York Times*, 2 January 2011.

the yuan to the US dollar and allow the Chinese currency to move more freely against a basket of currencies. The central bank said on the next day that it was determined to improve foreign exchange management and keep the yuan exchange rate at a reasonable and balanced level of basic stability, and safeguard macroeconomic and financial market stability.[2]

Since the announcement, the yuan has been trading in a gently upward trend against the dollar.[3] The announcement was made a week before the G20 Summit in Toronto, an indication of Chinese willingness to go some distance in meeting the demands of G20 members like the USA, the European Union, Brazil and India.[4] These countries had been calling on China to adopt a flexible exchange rate.

The decision did not come as a big surprise. There was much expectation in March 2010 that the Chinese central bank would make the announcement, but the crisis of the euro originating in Greece delayed it. As a result of the depreciation of the European currency, the yuan effectively appreciated against the euro, taking much of the heat off the European pressure.

The discussion on the yuan-dollar peg in March 2010 suggests a slight departure from past official practice. Speaking at the press conference in mid-March, Chinese Premier Wen Jiabao insisted that the yuan was not undervalued though he did not rule out a rise of the currency in the future. In a display of openness, the central bank favoured a rise of the yuan soon, a position different from Mr Wen's. Representing the interests of the exporters, the Commerce Ministry opposed a rise of the yuan.[5]

The Yuan in the Context of China's International Relations

The yuan exchange rate is one of the issues causing tension in China-US relations. In 2004–2005 when the Chinese current account surplus was increasingly rapidly, the US Congress pressed China for a large revaluation. After some initial resistance, China allowed its currency to rise within a narrow band in an upward trend. The yuan appreciated by 21 percent vis-à-vis the greenback from July 2005 to July 2008.

---

[2] "Yuan Story Different at Home", *International Herald Tribune*, 21 June 2010.

[3] X-rates.com, http://www.x-rates.com/cgi-bin/hlookup.cgi.

[4] "Beijing's Currency Decision Alters Focus of G-20", *International Herald Tribune*, 22 June 2010.

[5] "Chinese Officials Take Currency Tiff Public", *International Herald Tribune*, 26 March 2010.

With the outbreak of the 2008 financial crisis, China pegged the yuan to the dollar at the rate of 6.827. The crisis also led to a slump in Chinese exports to America. Meanwhile, China's huge domestic stimulus added to the global demand in 2009 and its trade surplus shrank sharply.[6]

Though very critical of China's refusal to let the yuan rise sharply, America has been keen to avoid a fierce confrontation with China for fear of stirring up a trade war. Coming so soon after the 2008 crisis, a trade war would do nobody any good. Instead it would slow down the economic recovery and hurt everybody at the same time. The bitter lessons of a trade war in the wake of the Great Depression in the 1930s are not so easily forgotten.

With the financial crisis over, America has plans to get out of the recession, to create jobs and to address its fiscal and trade imbalance. It wishes to reduce its trade deficit with China, and to increase its exports. The exchange rate of the yuan has become an obvious target. China appreciated the yuan in 2005, which America might think was due to its pressure. However, the currency appreciation did not lead to a drop in American imports from China.

The confrontation has added pressure to relations already strained by US arms sales to Taiwan, President Obama's meeting with the Dalai Lama and Beijing's dispute with Google over Internet censorship. The currency issue is not about a fundamental clash of national interests, but the product of domestic pressures.[7] President Obama is under pressure from labour unions while Chinese citizens are angered by what they perceive as American intimidation.

Besides the USA, the European Union, India, Brazil and the ASEAN member countries would also like to see a yuan appreciation. A few of these countries take a strong position like the USA; most of the others prefer to work behind the scenes.

Charges of Currency Manipulation

For some months, powerful voices in the USA have been pressuring China to let the yuan appreciate. Famous economists like Nobel laureate in economics Paul Krugman and 130 US congressmen argued that China kept the yuan

---

[6] "Yuan to Stay Cool", *International Herald Tribune*, 13 March 2010.
[7] Charles A. Kupchan, "Soothing China-U.S. Tensions", *The New York Times*, 31 March 2010.

artificially low in order to bolster its exports. A cheap yuan made it difficult to create jobs for the millions of unemployed Americans and for American companies to increase their exports. Even though most economists agree that the yuan is undervalued, there is no agreement as to the extent of the undervaluation. The figures provided by economists vary from less than 10 percent to 40 percent.[8]

There are three reasons why a revalued yuan would not bring about what these eminent economists and patriotic US congressmen wished for.[9] First, America's top exports to China are capital-intensive goods like aerospace and power-generation equipment. Price is but one of several factors for these purchases, along with technology, quality and service. In addition, American companies in those industries are usually competing against European and Japanese firms rather than Chinese manufacturers. Second, there is little direct competition between American and Chinese companies. The USA sells products like airplanes and pharmaceuticals while China sells electronics and textiles. Third, in response to a stronger yuan, companies would most likely shift labour-intensive production to Vietnam, Indonesia and other low-wage countries. US companies which need high-skilled jobs will continue to relocate abroad, as long as cheaper talent can be found in India and elsewhere. Together, these factors may explain why over the three years from 2005 to 2008, when the yuan appreciated nearly 20 percent against the dollar, American exports to China grew at a slightly slower pace than in the previous three-year period when the yuan did not appreciate at all (71 percent versus 89 percent).

So, the pressure on China in regard to the yuan issue is inspired by reasons other than economic rationality. Articulated at a time of high unemployment rates and a mid-term election in autumn 2010, the position taken by the congressmen was politically popular. Amidst such angry demands, the public did not hear the views of those US importers of Chinese goods and those US transnational companies which manufacture in China and export to the USA.

China denied the charge of currency manipulation. At a press conference in March, Premier Wen Jiabao said that the yuan was not undervalued. Representing the views of Chinese exporters, the Chinese Ministry of

---

[8]Fan Gang, "Renminbi and Reality", Project Syndicate, 23 March 2010, http://www. project-syndicate.org/commentary/fan13/English [accessed 7 April 2010].
[9]Mark Wu, "China's Currency Isn't Our Problem", *The New York Times*, 17 January 2011.

Commerce argued for maintaining the yuan-dollar peg.[10] However, the Chinese central bank said that the currency peg was a special response to the financial crisis, hinting that the fixed exchange rate was temporary. This was an open display of differences within the Beijing government — in itself interesting.

A Weak Yuan Benefits Certain Sections in American and China

In the midst of heated exchanges between China and the USA on yuan valuation, it is useful to note that a cheap yuan benefits ordinary American consumers of Chinese imports while it protects the jobs of labour-intensive and low-skilled manufacturing in China. Between 50 and 60 percent of US imports of Chinese manufactured goods are produced by foreign transnational companies in China; some of them are American companies.

A revalued yuan will reduce the volume of such imports, but will not mean sudden job creation for American workers. As pointed out by *The Economist*,[11] American factories no longer produce most of these products. The fall in Chinese imports will be made up for by imports from other low-cost producers from Asia and Latin America.

Reasons for the Yuan to Float

If we keep a distance from the politically charged exchanges, there are several sound economic reasons for China to revalue its currency. First, a move towards a more market-oriented exchange rate is in line with China's long march towards a market economy. In the past, China has shown a penchant for introducing market forces to stimulate its economic growth, e.g. by joining the WTO.

Second, China wants independence to set its own monetary policy in order to manage inflation and control asset bubbles. This can only happen if the yuan is no longer pegged to the greenback. Pegging the yuan to the dollar may thus be seen as a temporary measure adopted to deal with the uncertainties during the financial crisis.

Third, a strong yuan can nudge industries to upgrade their technologies. Low-tech companies will have to relocate. In high-value-adding sectors,

---

[10] "U.S. Puts Off Showdown with China on Yuan", *The International Herald Tribune*, 5 April 2010.
[11] "Yuan to Stay Cool", *The Economist*, 13 March 2010.

skills and technologies are much more important than exchange rates. There has been speculation that China's decision is motivated not so much by international trade concerns as it is by its greater strategy of industrial upgrading. Those who hold such views would cite Beijing's reluctance to suppress the recent labour unrest as an indication of China's new strategy.[12]

Fourth, China exercises control over currency flows, which can be used to block inflows of hot money. There are other instruments to stamp out and reduce the impact of hot money, e.g. increasing the amount of down payment for the purchase of real estate.

Fifth, the Chinese economy has been able to cope well with the 21 percent revaluation vis-à-vis the greenback from July 2005 to July 2008. A study by the Chinese Academy of Social Sciences (CASS) pointed out that a 1 percent appreciation of the yuan would impact exports negatively by 0.33 percent.[13] The yuan surged 15 percent against the euro within two months during autumn 2010 amidst the height of the debt problem in Europe.

Sixth, there are the obvious facts of robust exports and economic growth which underpin a strong currency. A strong yuan is good for China as it is cheaper to acquire natural resources and assets abroad. It also acts to reduce the impact of inflation as imported raw materials and consumer products will be cheaper in terms of Chinese currency. This point is very relevant to the Chinese authorities as inflation is again rearing its ugly head. The consumer price index in November 2011 reached a 28-month high of 5.1 percent, prompting the Chinese central bank to announce a hike in interest rates in December.[14] Part of the reason for the inflation is the quantitative easing in America.[15]

Seventh, holding down the value of the yuan does not come cheap for China. The Chinese central bank had to fork out 9.2 percent of the country's GDP to buy foreign reserves, mainly US Treasury securities that pay very low interest rates.[16] By aligning the yuan gradually closer to the market

[12] Behzad Yaghmaian, "Follow the Yuan", *International Herald Tribune*, 28 June 2010.
[13] Zhang Bin, "Expectation of Yuan Rise, Short-term Capital Flow and Its Impacts", Working Paper No. 2010W01, CASS Research Center for International Finance, 30 March 2010.
[14] "Taming Inflation High on Central Bank's Agenda", *China Daily*, 7 January 2011.
[15] "Borrowing Costs to Hit Two-Year High", *China Daily*, 7 January 2011.
[16] "Beijing to Weaken Yuan-Dollar Tie", *International Herald Tribune*, 9 April 2010.

condition, China would also move it closer to becoming part of the IMF's Special Drawing Rights basket of currencies.[17]

Eighth, a flexible exchange rate is one of the conditions for the internationalization of a currency. The other conditions are convertibility and a deep and liquid capital market. Since the outbreak of the global financial crisis, the Chinese government has shown enthusiasm for yuan internationalization. From the end of 2008 to August 2010, the People's Bank of China signed bilateral local currency swaps worth a total of 650 billion yuan with Korea, Hong Kong, Malaysia, Belarus, Indonesia and Argentina. Other moves in this direction are the issue of treasury bonds denominated in yuan in Hong Kong and permission for a list of coastal cities to use the yuan for cross-border trade settlement.[18]

On Its Own Terms

There are signs of inflation raising its ugly head. China is globally very competitive and exporters have more orders than they can fill.[19] Exporters in the coastal regions have had to increase their minimum wage by 20 percent in order to attract and retain workers to man their assembly lines.

The 8.7 percent and approximately 10 percent growth achieved in 2009 and 2010, respectively, were better than the critical figure of 8 percent needed to cope with the challenge of providing employment. China has weathered the financial crisis quite well. With the grave challenges posed by the crisis, the time has come for China to slowly move away from the fixed exchange rate to a more flexible exchange rate mechanism.

China does know the mechanisms of the global economy and its own fundamental economic interests. Foreign economists who know the Chinese economists advising the Chinese government can testify that the Chinese economists are very competent and knowledgeable.[20] This fact is likely to feature in the thinking of US Treasury officials who decline to follow the open confrontation approach of US lawmakers in raising the currency issue with their Chinese counterparts.

---

[17] "Yuan May Join Global Currency Basket", *The Asahi Shimbun,* 1 July 2010, http://www.asahi.com/english/TKY201006300452.html [accessed 1 July 2010].

[18] Zhang Ming, "The Impacts of Global Financial Crisis on Chinese Foreign Exchange Reserves and China's Responses", Working Paper No. 2010W13, Research Center for International Finance, 2010.

[19] "Chinese Officials Take Currency Tiff Public", *International Herald Tribune,* 26 March 2010.

[20] Richard C. Koo, *The Holy Grail of Macroeconomics* (Singapore: Wiley, 2009).

It is crucially important to note that China has revalued its currency on its own terms, and this approach is going to endure. It is rewarding to recall China's decision not to devalue its currency during the Asian financial crisis though the move could have boosted its exports. While the decision was praised by then US President Bill Clinton, Beijing certainly did not do so to win kudos from the good president. The refusal to devalue the yuan was intended to help Hong Kong hold on to its fixed exchange rate with the US dollar and not to aggravate the problems confronted by its East Asian neighbours. Another reason was that devaluation would fuel inflation at home.[21]

Judging from past practices of the Chinese government, China will let the yuan move within a narrow band in an upward trend so that the impact will not be beyond control. The track record of China during the period of economic reform has shown that it is able to pick up lessons from other countries. It is safe to say that China will not repeat the mistake of Japan at the 1985 Plaza Accord when it sharply appreciated the Japanese yen.

According to the CASS study, the most adverse impact of yuan appreciation is that it may set off a new evaluation of assets in the capital market. The combination of a sharp yuan appreciation and loose monetary policy in the context of a robust economic recovery may lead to an asset bubble.[22]

In fact, as a result of rising labour costs, much of the low-margin and labour-intensive manufacturing in China has moved out of China to countries with cheaper labour. High-tech companies may even favour a dearer yuan. The migration of labour-intensive factories out of China will free up labour for them. Imports will also be cheaper.

Some American politicians may like to argue that China revalued its currency in 2005 under American prodding. Even if this were true, China today is no longer the China of six years ago. It has weathered the global financial meltdown very well. By using a huge fiscal stimulus to maintain high growth, it has played a positive role in the global recovery, a fact

---

[21] Hongying Wang, "Dangers and Opportunities: The Implications of the Asian Financial Crisis for China", in Gregory Noble and John Ravenhill (eds.), *The Asian Financial Crisis and the Architecture of Global Finance* (Cambridge: Cambridge University Press, 2000). Gerald Tan, *The Asian Currency Crisis* (Singapore: Times Academic Press, 2000).

[22] Zhang Bin, "Expectation of Yuan Rise, Short-term Capital Flow and Its Impacts", Working Paper No. 2010W01, CASS Research Center for International Finance, 30 March 2010.

highly appreciated by its Asian neighbours. And every Chinese knows that China is the biggest creditor of America. Noisy pressure from America is thus counterproductive as it stokes up Chinese nationalism.

Professor Charles Kupchan of Georgetown University understands the problem well when he says, "Washington is right to want a revaluation of the yuan, but wrong to pursue that objective through bullying Beijing."[23] Instead of open confrontation and pressure, a much better way is to raise the issue in closed-door meetings of government leaders and finance ministers.

As pointed out by Joseph Stiglitz, the very concept of currency manipulation itself is flawed. He says, "[A]ll governments take actions that directly or indirectly affect the exchange rate. Reckless budget deficits can lead to a weak currency; so can low interest rates. Until the recent crisis in Greece, the US benefited from a weak dollar/euro exchange rate. Should Europeans have accused the US of 'manipulating' the exchange rate to expand exports at its expense?"[24]

Beyond the Issue of Exchange Rates

The rationale for the USA and Europe in pressuring China on the exchange rate issue is to redress trade imbalances. But a gradual appreciation of the yuan is not likely to solve the problem. The exchange rate is a minor factor in high-tech exports, and even a sharp rise in the exchange rate is unlikely to hamper high-tech exports. This point is amply illustrated by the Japanese experience. Even low-tech exporters can learn to adjust to the challenge, e.g. by moving to a low-cost production area.

Many factors other than the exchange rate affect a country's trade balance. A key determinant is national savings. America's multilateral trade deficit will not be significantly narrowed until it saves significantly more; while the Great Recession has induced higher household savings (which were near zero), this has been more than offset by the increased government deficit.[25] Another long-term solution of the trade imbalance must come from the Chinese consuming more and saving less.[26]

---

[23] Charles A. Kupchan, "Soothing China-U.S. Tensions", *The New York Times*, 31 March 2010.
[24] Joseph Stiglitz, "No Time for a Trade War", Project Syndicate, 6 April 2010, www. project-syndicate.org/commentary/stiglitz124/English [accessed 7 April 2010].
[25] ibid.
[26] Calla Wiemer, "Don't Revalue the Yuan Yet", *Wall Street Journal*, 7 January 2010.

The exchange rate is not the most central factor in achieving a sustainable rebalancing in China's foreign trade. "A surplus of exports over imports is simply the external manifestation of an excess of savings over domestic investment. Export revenues not spent on imports are used to acquire foreign assets, which represent Chinese savings invested abroad."[27] China cannot escape its international responsibility to redress global trade imbalances. But it cannot carry out this task alone. Other countries with huge surpluses are Japan, Germany and Saudi Arabia — all members of the G20 — and between them, they have to play their part.

Rather than focusing on the exchange rate issue, Washington would do well to follow another approach to increase its exports. For example, it can loosen the restrictions on technology exports to the emerging economies. It would increase American exports to willing customers. Except for high technology that has clear military application, there is no strong case in the context of globalization and the market economy for the USA to restrict high-tech exports.[28] High technology will also help China move away from labour-intensive manufacturing and speed up the use of environmental friendly technologies.

Turning Threats of Currency War into Economic Recovery[29]

As we mentioned earlier, the mutual recrimination between China and the USA raises the ugly spectre of a currency war. Should it happen, it would greatly damage the global promise of constructive cooperation and interdependence.

Can the threats of a currency war morph into something more benign? Better still, can they stimulate fresh ideas and moves that lead to a robust global economic recovery? The answer is yes if we follow the idea of win-win business deals, and use it with imagination and goodwill. The simplest way out is for China and other countries with huge foreign reserves to buy American high-tech and business assets.

But what happens if the USA restricts sales of the goods and assets that foreign companies want to buy? The USA has banned the export of

---

[27]Calla Wiemer, "Don't Revalue the Yuan Yet", *Wall Street Journal*, 7 January 2010.
[28]Michael Heng Siam-Heng and Lim Tai Wei, *Destructive Creativity of Wall Street and the East Asian Response* (Singapore: World Scientific, 2009).
[29]This section is a slightly edited version of an op-ed piece by the authors which appeared as "Increasing High-tech Trade" in *China Daily* on 7 January 2011.

high-end semiconductor plants to China. In 2005, the United States blocked the takeover bid by Chinese oil company CNOOC for American oil company Unocal. Many global energy experts were not convinced that the proposed deal could affect petroleum availability or endanger US security. And China is not alone in facing such restrictions from the USA. A Middle Eastern country was not allowed to buy a port facility. The reason, given in plain language, is that the USA does not consider these countries as friends and therefore cannot trust them.

Let us for a moment leave aside the question of whether it is wise for the USA to impose such restrictions. Washington may need more time to convince itself of the "historic potential of productive American-Chinese cooperation", to borrow a phrase from Zbigniew Brzezinski.[30] Let us turn our minds to ask if there are other ways to solve the problem. Europe has many things that the USA has. But unlike the USA, there is no central political power to restrict the export of a given technology or to disallow the sale of assets to foreign buyers. This provides a more favourable environment for buyers from Asia to conduct business transactions.

China, with its vast pool of engineering and scientific expertise, does not always need to buy the most advanced technologies. There are two advantages of not going for the very best: it is cheaper and it faces much less official restriction in export. China can use its technical skills to improve on the technologies, as it has done in the case of high-speed rail.

For their part, the sellers of European technologies can use the cash to acquire top-end technological assets in the USA, where they face less opposition or even no opposition. With this approach, we end up with a situation where the trade imbalance between China and the USA is reduced.

Thus, the US economy can be given a more solid foundation on which to recover and the greenback can bounce back, while Europe benefits from its role as a global trader of technologies. China will no longer need to worry so much about the shrinking worth of its dollar reserves. At the same time, it will have access to a vast range of technologies. The arrangement would be a win-win situation for the whole world. For the parties concerned, it would have a wider mission than national self-interest. One may even say that such a collaboration would carry with it a moral imperative of the new century of deep and unprecedented globalization.

---

[30]Zbigniew Brzezinski (2011) "How to Stay Friends With China", *New York Times*, 2 January 2011.

Thinking along this line, China may wish to consider acquiring business assets in Europe. As an example, China did a good job by investing in the port facilities in Greece, a welcome move for the Greek economy in a difficult moment. In the current situation, there is scope for China to widen and deepen its economic relationships with other euro countries in trouble. An essential point to note in this context is that China has to beef up its ability to do this kind of overseas deals. The track record of Chinese firms in this field has not been too encouraging. Rather than retreating as a reaction to some failures, there is more urgency and need to acquire the skills to do a better job in this area of international business.

Moreover, there are long-term benefits of investing in production facilities in European Union member countries in Eastern Europe. While helping to boost the economy and to provide jobs, Chinese companies can gain direct access to the European Union market. This would follow the approach of Japan. A few decades ago, in response to the threat of protectionism against Japanese goods, Japanese firms like Toyota relocated some of their manufacturing to the USA.

A robust economic recovery of the US economy is in the interests of the world. In this sense, Asia should play a positive role in helping to speed up the recovery. The same applies to Europe. At the same time, Washington should do its part in making the whole process easier for everybody. It is essential for it to note that it is in its own interests to do so. A huge trade deficit is a symptom of a serious disease of the real economy. With a robust revival of the real economy, the trade deficit will evaporate in the fullness of time.

Finally, there is a political benefit for all if there is deepening and widening economic cooperation between Europe and Asia. After the end of World War II, the USA emerged as one of the two superpowers. But since the demise of its challenger, the Soviet Union, at the end of the Cold War, the USA has become the sole superpower, or more accurately, the hyperpower. According to Amy Chua, a hyperpower is more than a superpower, in the sense that it is a power unchallenged in the military, economic, technological, cultural and political fields.[31] Such an enviable position is a seductive invitation to hubris and unilateralism, leading easily to foreign policy blunders and military adventures.[32] Taking a realistic

---

[31] Amy Chua, *Day of Empire: How Hyperpowers Rise to Global Dominance — and Why They Fall* (New York: Doubleday, 2007).
[32] Gideon Rose, *How Wars End* (New York: Simon & Schuster, 2010).

view of the current global situation, the most likely candidate to exercise meaningful restraint on the USA is Europe. Unfortunately, events since 9/11 have shown that Europe by itself sometimes cannot do very much to deter Uncle Sam from his unilateralism and reckless pursuit of what he considers his core interests. With a helping hand from Asia on the rise, Europe is in a better position to persuade its dear friend to take others' advice more seriously in the furtherance of global issues like global warming and organized crime. There is a significant body of enlightened and liberal opinion in the USA itself which will welcome such restraints on America's unilateral actions.

Chapter Five

Promoting China-ASEAN Economic Cooperation

Introduction

With the advent of China's economic reform three decades ago, trade and investment between ASEAN and China have been increasing year by year. The Asian financial crisis of 1997 acted as a catalyst to widen and deepen the relationship. There was also a strong move at the highest official level on both sides to speed up the process and degree of economic cooperation. The most significant of this was the initiative to set up the China-ASEAN Free Trade Agreement (CAFTA), which formally came into being on 1 January 2010. The agreement gave birth to the largest FTA in terms of population (1.9 billion), with a combined GDP of US$5.6 trillion and total trade volume of US$4.5 trillion. It is the third largest trading block after the European Union and the North American Free Trade Agreement region in terms of GDP. CAFTA has not disappointed its well-wishers. The first seven months of 2010 saw China's exports to ASEAN go up by 43.2 percent while ASEAN's exports to China grew by 56.1 percent when compared to the same period in the previous year.

Besides trade, CAFTA represents a set of huge opportunities for the members of this huge geographical region and economy to increase their cooperation in the areas of investment and infrastructure development. This point takes on extra significance in the aftermath of the 2008 financial crisis.

Rapid Growth of China-ASEAN Trade in the CAFTA Preparatory Years

Ever since ASEAN as a group and China established official contact in 1991, the two sides have made remarkable progress in forging a strategic partnership for peace and prosperity (see Table 5.1). This is manifested in their cooperation in trade, investment and other issues of mutual interest, ranging from maritime security to non-traditional security challenges. Trade and economic ties have enjoyed robust growth after the signing of

Table 5.1.   Major activities leading up to CAFTA implementation.

1991	Chinese Foreign Minister Qian Qichen attended the opening session of the 24th ASEAN Ministerial Meeting in Kuala Lumpur. China expressed its keen interest to forge a cooperation with ASEAN for mutual benefit.
1995	ASEAN and China established the ASEAN-China Joint Science and Technology Committee to plan, approve, coordinate, monitor and evaluate joint cooperative programmes and activities. Since then, there have been many joint programmes and activities convened.
1996	China was accorded full Dialogue Partner status at the 29th ASEAN Ministerial Meeting in Jakarta, Indonesia.
1997	Chinese President Jiang Zemin and ASEAN leaders had their first informal summit and issued a joint statement to establish a partnership of good neighbourliness and mutual trust oriented towards the 21st century.
2000	Chinese Premier Zhu Rongji proposed setting up an FTA with ASEAN.
2001	ASEAN and China formally agreed to set up a China-ASEAN Free Trade Agreement in ten years' time.
2002	Signing of the Framework Agreement on Comprehensive Economic Cooperation in November 2002 to establish the China-ASEAN Free Trade Area (CAFTA). Since then, trade and economic ties between ASEAN and China have grown rapidly.
2003	Signing of Joint Declaration of the Heads of State/Government of the ASEAN Nations and China on Strategic Partnership for Peace and Prosperity at the 7th ASEAN-China Summit.
2004	Adopted five-year (2005–2010) Plan of Action to implement the Joint Declaration at the 8th ASEAN-China Summit. The Plan has served as the master plan to broaden and deepen ASEAN-China dialogue relations in a comprehensive and mutually beneficial manner with a view to strengthening the strategic partnership for regional peace, development and prosperity.
2004–2005	The Agreements on Trade in Goods and Dispute Settlement Mechanism between ASEAN and China were signed in November 2004, and implemented in July 2005.
2006	ASEAN and China celebrated 15 years of dialogue relations with the Commemorative Summit Marking the 15th Anniversary of ASEAN-China Dialogue Relations in Nanning, China. The Summit issued a Joint Statement to further strengthen ASEAN-China relations towards an enhanced strategic partnership.
2007	The Agreements on Trade in Services of the Framework Agreement on Comprehensive Economic Co-operation between ASEAN and China were signed in January and came into force on 1 July.
2009	The ASEAN-China Investment Agreement was signed during the 41st ASEAN Economic Ministers Meeting. This completed the ASEAN-China negotiation processes on the FTA as set out in the Framework Agreement on Comprehensive Economic Cooperation between ASEAN and China.
2010	Implementation of CAFTA in January.

Source: Official website of the Association of Southeast Asian Nations, http://www.aseansec.org/index2008.html [accessed 12 May 2010].

the Framework Agreement on Comprehensive Economic Cooperation in November 2002 to establish the China-ASEAN Free Trade Area.[1] China and ASEAN adopted an incremental approach to the FTA. Both sides started to implement the CAFTA's Trade in Goods Agreement with import tariff reductions from July 2005, with the five-year tariff reduction schedule entirely phased in from January 2010. The average tariff on ASEAN exports to China was slashed to 0.1 percent in 2010, while the average tariff on China exports to older ASEAN-6 members was slashed to 0.6 percent. Currently, around 7,000 items traded between China and ASEAN are zero-rated. By 2015, the policy of a zero-tariff rate for 90 percent of traded goods is expected to apply between China and the remaining four ASEAN members.[2] Because of such tariff-lowering measures, many tariffs were already very low before 2010.[3] CAFTA may therefore be seen as a formalization of what has been going on for a decade.

CAFTA is an initiative to enhance economic regional integration, and like other such initiatives, it has its economic and political background. The economic imperatives presented themselves in the form of the 1997 Asian financial crisis and the changes brought about by China's accession to the World Trade Organization. Relatively unaffected by the 1997 crisis, China was able to continue doing business with Southeast Asian countries badly affected by the crisis. What was more important, it kept its promise not to devalue the Chinese currency. Between them, these factors gave ASEAN countries a positive impression of China. It was a contrast to the bullying behaviour of the IMF which was widely believed to be a proxy of Washington.[4] The political lesson was easy to learn.

The 1997 Asian financial crisis prompted East Asian economies to increase their cooperation and they sought common ground to guard against future crises. In 2000, ASEAN, China, Japan and South Korea launched a multilateral pact on currency swaps, known as the Chiang Mai Initiative, to pool their foreign reserves to help crisis-ridden East Asian countries.

With China joining the WTO in 2001, more transnational companies set up their production facilities in mainland China. Happening soon after the 1997 financial crisis, it made a lot of sense for Southeast Asian countries to broaden and deepen their trade with China. Besides being attracted to

---

[1] "ASEAN-China Dialogue Relations", http://www.aseansec.org/5874.htm [accessed 10 May 2010].
[2] http://news.163.com//1010101/001SRTDIVEM000/20Gu.html.
[3] "Asia's Never-Closer Union", *The Economist*, 4 February 2010.
[4] Lam Peng Er, "The Asian Financial Crisis and Its Impact on Regional Order: Opening Pandora's Box", *The Journal of Pacific Asia*, Vol. 6 (2000), pp. 57–80.

the economic potential of China's rapid growth and liberalization, they could become suppliers to feed the global production network centred in China. The final manufactured goods would then be exported mainly to Europe and the USA from China. All these happened in the context of globalization, with regional cooperation as part of the "game". Three crucial rationales have been identified by Kevin Cai. First, CAFTA is a response to the intensified regionalism elsewhere. Second, the FTA helps to cement the growing economic ties between ASEAN and China. Third, the FTA helps to coordinate government policies — a point made very clear in the Asian financial crisis.[5]

From the Chinese side, there is an acute recognition that its economic well-being depends critically on a peaceful and stable global environment. Its embrace of globalization means the need to do more business with the outside world, especially its neighbours. It is also keen to ensure a reliable source of raw materials. The end of 2001 was a good time for China to broach the idea of an FTA to ASEAN: "The timing is ideal, as the United States is distracted by the war on terror, Iraq, Iran, and North Korea, while Southeast Asia is still grappling with the aftermath of the 1997–8 Asian Financial Crisis."[6] With America distracted and Japan weakened by its long recession, China's pragmatic approach of increasing trade and investment has won much goodwill in the region.[7] It may be added that by excluding Taiwan, CAFTA benefits China as it isolates Taiwan, a bonus point for China's long-term project of reunification. This incidentally reveals the fact that economic and political matters are closely intertwined. This is true of CAFTA, as it is true of other free trade agreements. China needs the political goodwill of its Southeast Asian neighbours as much as the neighbours want to profit from strengthening economic ties with China.[8]

In August 2009, China and ASEAN ratified the China-ASEAN Investment Agreement during the 41st ASEAN Economic Ministers Meeting.

---

[5]Kevin G. Cai, "The ASEAN-China Free Trade Agreement and East Asian Regional Grouping", *Contemporary Southeast Asia*, Vol. 25 (2003), pp. 387–404.

[6]Vincent Wei-cheng Wang, "The Logic of China-ASEAN Free Trade Agreement: Economic Statecraft of 'Peaceful Rise'", Paper presented at the China in the World, the World in China International Conference, "Implications of a Transforming China: Domestic, Regional and Global Impacts", University of Malaya, Kuala Lumpur, 5–6 August 2007, http://ics.um.edu.my/images/ics/aug2007/vincentw.pdf.

[7]Joshua Kurlantzick, *Charm Offensive: How China's Soft Power Is Transforming the World* (New Haven: Yale University Press, 2007).

[8]The authors are grateful to an anonymous reviewer for pointing this out.

This, together with the already signed China-ASEAN Agreements on Trade in Goods and Services, completed the negotiation process of CAFTA. It paved the way for the implementation of CAFTA from January 2010 for China and the older ASEAN members (i.e. Brunei, Indonesia, Malaysia, the Philippines, Singapore and Thailand). The FTA between China and the newer ASEAN members (Cambodia, Laos, Myanmar and Vietnam) will only take effect from January 2015.

As a free trade agreement, CAFTA is quite comprehensive as it covers trade in goods and services as well as investment. The new agreement has created the largest FTA in terms of population (1.9 billion), with a combined GDP of US$5.6 trillion and total trade volume of US$4.5 trillion. It is the third largest trading block after the European Union and North American Free Trade Agreement region in terms of GDP.[9] CAFTA is expected to boost China-ASEAN trade alongside expanding intra-industry trade and increase investment flows between the two sides.[10] Because of the enlarged market, it is likely to attract more FDI to the region.

Since 1991, China-ASEAN trade has experienced significant growth. From 1991 to 2000, the total China-ASEAN trade volume grew at an annual rate of more than 15 percent from US$8 billion to US$40 billion. After China joined the WTO in 2001, the total China-ASEAN trade volume grew at an even faster pace. During the period from 2001 to 2008, China-ASEAN trade ballooned at an annual rate of over 20 percent from US$42 billion to over US$230 billion (see Figure 5.1). China is now ASEAN's third largest trading partner. To a certain extent, the rapid expansion of China-ASEAN trade since 2001 was partly due to the "early harvest" programme of CAFTA, which liberalized China's agricultural market to ASEAN countries.

While working towards CAFTA, ASEAN redoubled its efforts to create not only free trade amongst its members, but also an ASEAN Economic Community by 2015 in which goods, skilled labour and capital could move freely. The 2008 financial crisis gave this another boost.[11]

---

[9] Keynote speech by ASEAN Deputy Secretary-General, 7 January 2010.

[10] "China-ASEAN Free Trade Area (CAFTA) — Implications for Hong Kong's Merchandise Exports", 8 March 2010, http://www.hktdc.com/info/mi/a/ef/en/1X06OJ4B/1/ Economic-Forum/China-ASEAN-Free-Trade-Area–CAFTA–%E2%80%93-Implications-for-Hong-Kong%E2%80%99s-Merchandise-Exports.htm [accessed 22 April 2010].

[11] "Asia's Never-Closer Union", *The Economist*, 4 February 2010.

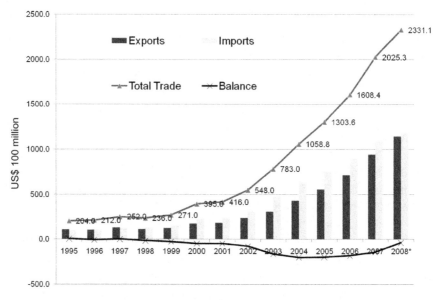

Figure 5.1.   China-ASEAN trade, 1995–2008.
Source: China Statistical Yearbook 2009.

China-centric Regional Production Network

A strong factor behind the growth of China-ASEAN trade was the integration of ASEAN economies into the China-centric regional production network. The China-centric regional production network was formed towards the end of the 1990s when China began to assume the region's traditional position of a manufacturing and assembly hub (mostly for labour-intensive and lower-value-added products as shown in Figure 5.2). Some of the conditions that allowed China to take on this role include its limited exposure to the Asian financial crisis of 1997, its ability to attract FDI away from the ASEAN region, and its large pool of cheap labour. To regain its competitiveness, ASEAN economies leveraged on China's new-found role by aligning themselves more closely with the processing phase of China's production. This is illustrated by the composition of ASEAN exports to China from the late 1990s onwards. On the one hand, raw materials and intermediate manufacture products have remained the top commodities in ASEAN's exports to China over the years. On the other hand, ASEAN countries have upgraded their export structure based on their evolving comparative advantage by shifting focus to high-value-added intermediate products. Indeed, the share

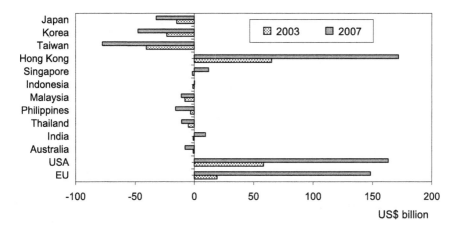

Figure 5.2.   China's trade balance with selected countries, 2003 and 2007.
Source: China Statistical Yearbook 2008.

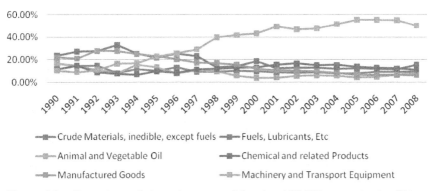

Figure 5.3.   Percentage of top six commodities in ASEAN's exports to China,
1995–2008.
Source: The official website of the Association of Southeast Asian Nations, www.aseansec.
org.

of resource-based commodities decreased from two thirds of the total export
value of ASEAN to China in the early 1990s to only 22 percent in 1999,
and has remained almost at the same level ever since. Meanwhile, the
relative share of intermediate manufacture goods (machinery and transport
equipment, as shown in Figure 5.3) — electrical machinery, computer chips
and automobile parts particularly — went up drastically from 12 percent in
1990 to 52 percent in 2008. This economic arrangement between China and

ASEAN complemented the export-oriented strategy of both sides. ASEAN economies would supply the raw materials and intermediate products for China's manufacturing, while China would export the finished product to third countries. Based on the economic performance of ASEAN and China in recent years, it seems that this production network was able to usher in a period of strong growth for both sides.

However, this changed after the financial meltdown in September 2008. The global financial crisis has cut back Western demand for Chinese exports, which in turn reduces ASEAN export of processing materials to China. This has had an immediate impact on the economic growth of both ASEAN and China.

It is likely that global demand, especially from the Western economies, will remain weak despite improvement in the global economy. This is because the improvement is mainly due to aggressive government stimulus packages and a correction in private sector inventories. There is yet to be a firm or sustainable rebound in private spending. This is not a surprising development as unemployment rates remain high and the credit market continues to remain tight in developed economies.

High-spending consumers in the United States and developed European countries are now saving money and paying off debts, while banks are building reserves and hoarding cash. The change in consumer behaviour in the developed markets has in turn affected the global economy. Thriftiness on the part of Western consumers has led to a collapse of the bottomless appetite for goods that are made from components and raw materials from Asian, African and Latin American countries and assembled in China. In the face of this changing world order, it is necessary for China and ASEAN to revise their roles in the global economy in order to ensure a continuation of their economic development.

The launch of CAFTA brought new hopes to this area. However, there are some challenges that cannot be ignored. On 21 April 2010, China's Vice-Minister of Commerce Yi Xiaozhun said China-ASEAN bilateral trade had grown rapidly in the first three months of 2010 compared with the same period in the previous year. China's exports to ASEAN went up 46.7 percent while ASEAN's exports to China grew even more, by 76.6 percent.[12] The high growth of this two-sided trade is not necessarily due entirely to the

---

[12] "CAFTA Passes First Test, Registers Higher Trade with Asean", Bernama, 21 April 2010, http://www.bernama.com/bernama/v5/newsbusiness.php?id=492464 [accessed 22 April 2010].

launch of CAFTA at the beginning of the year. To illustrate this point, let us look at China's trade figures with non-CAFTA countries. China's imports from Australia increased by 64 percent, Japan by 56 percent and South Korea by 61 percent in the same period.[13] The numbers would have been smaller had it not been for the slump in previous trade due to the recent financial crisis. For example, ASEAN exported 8.8 percent less to China in 2009.[14]

Some Challenges

Like any other FTA, CAFTA has its winners and losers, its opportunities and challenges. Success brings with it some problems, which need to be handled rationally and carefully. Concretely, CAFTA has revealed the following issues: trade deficits, pressures felt by some ASEAN industries, market size constrained by income, and competition from other FTAs.

Trade Deficits in ASEAN Countries

From 2001 to 2006, at a time when the volume of ASEAN-China trade was booming, there was more or less trade balance, with ASEAN enjoying some surplus. The situation began to change in the last few years. Vietnam and Indonesia have been showing trade deficits, and the gap seems to be increasing. According to data provided by ASEAN, the ASEAN side showed a trade deficit of US$21.5 billion in 2008. According to the Chinese Ministry of Commerce, China's trade with ASEAN registered a decrease in deficit from more than US$20 billion in 2004 to US$2.8 billion in 2008. During the first three quarters of 2009, China had a surplus of US$90 million in its trade with ASEAN.

As Figure 5.3 shows, almost half of ASEAN's exports to China are resources and agricultural products. Compared to the manufacturing products ASEAN imports from China, its exports to China have low value-added content and less potential for future development.

Moreover, there is the issue of exchange rates. So far in 2010, the Malaysian ringgit is up 7.5 percent against the dollar and the Indonesian rupiah is up 4 percent. As long as the yuan is pegged to the dollar, the

---

[13] "An Appetite that Changes the World", *International Herald Tribune*, 27 April 2010.
[14] "CAFTA Passes First Test, Registers Higher Trade with Asean", Bernama, 21 April 2010, http://www.bernama.com/bernama/v5/newsbusiness.php?id=492464 [accessed 22 April 2010].

appreciation of ASEAN currencies makes their products more expensive for Chinese importers. Such exchange rate movements may accentuate the trade deficits. The dollar and yuan are now equally important in Asia. It can be expected that ASEAN countries will have larger trade deficits with China if no drastic steps are taken to reverse the trend.

It must be added that most ASEAN countries do not have a big buffer of foreign reserves. Trade deficits, especially when they show signs of rapid increase, weaken the countries' capacity to import. At the same time, it increases currency risks and lowers the countries' ability to cope with the flow of hot money.

Pressures Experienced by Some ASEAN Industries

The economic structures of ASEAN countries and China have both complementary and competitive aspects. Having a huge population of 1.3 billion, China has the task of providing employment for its vast pool of labour force. At its existing level of modernization, its labour-intensive industries will remain a mainstay of employment in the foreseeable future. Unlike Japan and South Korea, China cannot afford to relocate all its labour-intensive industries like home appliances manufacturing to ASEAN countries.

In early January, soon after CAFTA came into force, its impact was covered by newspapers in Indonesia, the Philippines, Malaysia, Thailand and Singapore. While reporting on the positive aspects, they expressed concern that cheap Chinese products like textile products, footwear, headgear and bags might drive such industries in ASEAN to the wall.

There are voices in Indonesia and the Philippines which have championed the cause of such industries, especially textiles.[15] The Indonesian Textile Association in Indonesia said that they had witnessed the closure of 271 textile factories due to competition from China in 2008 and 2009. The spokesperson of the Indonesian Ministry of Industry revealed that the Indonesian government had written to ASEAN to ask for a postponement to 2011 of zero tariffs for textile, steel and chemicals, to

---

[15]Walden Bello, "The China-Asean Free Trade Area: Propaganda and Reality", Inquirer, 14 January 2010, http://opinion.inquirer.net/viewpoints/columns/view/20100114-247344/The-China-Asean-Free-Trade-Area-Propaganda-and-Reality [accessed 24 April 2010]; "Is China-ASEAN Free Trade Agreement — CAFTA Necessary to Renegotiate?", Voice of Indonesia, http://en.voi.co.id/voi-dignitorial/773-is-china-asean-free-trade-agreement-cafta-necessary-to-renegotiate.html [accessed 24 April 2010].

give Indonesian enterprises more time to adjust. The Indonesian Minister of Trade, while assuring that Indonesia would abide by CAFTA, would set up a government agency to follow closely the impact of the FTA on Indonesian industries. The suggestion is that Indonesia may resort to non-tariff measures to safeguard its enterprises, such as complicated and time-consuming import procedures and quality control. In fact, Indonesia has imposed the requirement that China's products can only be imported via ten specified ports.

Market Size Constrained by Income

Though ASEAN has a vast population, its purchasing power is relatively weak. The average annual income is slightly above US$2,000. The older ASEAN-6 fares better with an average annual income of US$4,000–5,000. During its best years of economic development from 2004 to 2008, the GDP registered an annual growth of 5.8 percent while the level of consumption increased more slowly.

The low rate of consumption increase is due to the low rate of income growth, which in turn is due to low productivity and employment opportunities. The traditional approach to boost employment was through export-oriented industrialization. However, with the current recession, technological advances and production overcapacity worldwide, it has become much more difficult for latecomers to rely on export-oriented and labour-intensive industries to provide employment.

To raise productivity, it is necessary to develop basic infrastructure and to speed up the transfer of technology and skills to ASEAN, especially to the new members. This means FDI from the advanced countries. Take the case of Indonesia with its workforce of 110 million and population of 230 million. The unemployment rate is 8.1 percent, which in itself is not high. But of this employment, only 30 percent are in government or corporate firms. The remaining 70 percent work in the agricultural sector, as taxi drivers or are self-employed as small-business people. From 1995 to 2008, the increase in labour supply exceeded the increase in employment by 2 percent. It is estimated that 17 percent of the people are in absolute poverty, surviving on less than US$1.5 per day.

In the Philippines, the situation is worse. According to official statistics, the unemployment rate in July 2009 was 7.6 percent, and the under-employment rate 19.8 percent. The total number of unemployed and under-employed was 12 million. The country suffered from an export slump, reduced remittance from Filipinos working abroad and a drop in FDI. At the same time, its population of 90 million increases at 2.4 percent per year, the most in Asia and higher than the government target of 1.9 percent.

Competition from Other FTAs

ASEAN has signed FTAs with its various partners. All of them aim at tariff reduction. CAFTA is the first to come into force. The other FTAs are with Japan, South Korea, India, Australia and New Zealand. In its trade relations with ASEAN, China has to compete with these countries. In 2007 and 2008, China's trade volume with ASEAN exceeded Japan's with ASEAN, but in 2009, Japan's trade volume with ASEAN overtook China's. China's imports from Singapore, Malaysia, Indonesia and Vietnam are more than Japan's but its imports from the Philippines and Thailand are less than Japan's. The main components of both China's and Japan's exports to ASEAN are electronic/electrical goods and machinery, but Japanese goods are of higher quality. Japanese cars have captured a stable market in the ASEAN region. Japanese corporations have a longer history of trade with and investment in ASEAN and enjoy much goodwill. Recently, Japan initiated the Japan-Mekong Region Ministerial Meeting and convened the Japan-Mekong Summit. To counter China's influence in Southeast Asia, Japan proposed the ASEAN-Japan Comprehensive Economic Partnership. The agreement was signed by both sides in April 2008 and came into effect in December 2008.

While ASEAN countries want to gain from the rapid economic development in China and India, they are also cautious of the implications of the rise of the new powers. They therefore see value in the institutions and mechanism of the 10 + 8 (the ten ASEAN members, China, Japan, South Korea, India, Australia, New Zealand, Russia and the USA) as checks and balances and to reduce the adverse impact of deepening cooperation among China, Japan and South Korea in Northeast Asia.

As part of this trend, Brunei, Chile, New Zealand and Singapore set up the Trans-Pacific Strategic Economic Partnership (TPP) in 2005.[16] Since then it has expanded to include the United States, Australia, Peru and Vietnam. The TPP is now one of the Obama administration's main trade

---

[16] "Trans-Pacific Strategic Economic Partnership Agreement", New Zealand Ministry of Foreign Affairs and Trade, http://www.mfat.govt.nz/Trade-and-Economic-Relations/ Trade-Agreements/Trans-Pacific/index.php [accessed 13 May 2010].

policies with its five-year goal of doubling US exports. At the same time, America is intensely aware of China's dominance in East Asian trade and the TPP provides a platform for the USA to respond to it.[17]

Making Use of New Opportunities

CAFTA features in many discussions on how China and ASEAN should respond to the 2008 financial crisis. Much of these revolve around the reality of shrinking Western markets and the need to increase intra-regional trade. CAFTA means a bigger market, as producers have a larger and more integrated market, leading to better economies of scale, higher efficiency and economic growth. Product differentiation and economies of scale are expected to grow over time and the role of the region as an integrated production base for the global supply chain will also be strengthened. If history can act as a guide, CAFTA will stimulate trade growth, and this is confirmed by data so far. For example, in the first seven months of 2010, China's exports to ASEAN went up by 43.2 percent while ASEAN's exports to China grew by 56.1 percent compared to the same period in the previous year. While CAFTA members are naturally expected to benefit from trade creation, trade with non-members might decline. CAFTA's impact on individual non-member economies is likely to vary drastically, depending on how well a non-member is linked individually to signatory members in terms of trade, supply chains and other business arrangements.[18]

CAFTA opens up new avenues for ASEAN's and China's business community to expand their business. Prior to the global financial crisis, economic growth and development in the ASEAN and China region benefited the MNCs more than the business community of ASEAN. In fact, intra-ASEAN investment only accounted for a small percentage of ASEAN's total FDI. Of the US$63 billion of FDI coming into ASEAN in 2007, intra-ASEAN FDI only amounted to US$10 billion or about 15 percent of ASEAN's total FDI inflow. China's investment in ASEAN was

---

[17]Bernard K. Gordon, "America Misses Another Asian Opportunity", *The Wall Street Journal*, 23 April 2010.

[18] "China-ASEAN Free Trade Area (CAFTA) — Implications for Hong Kong's Merchandise Exports", Hong Kong Trade Development Council, 8 March 2010, http://www.hktdc.com/info/mi/a/ef/en/1X06OJ4B/1/Economic-Forum/China-ASEAN-Free-Trade-Area–CAFTA–%E2%80%93-Implications-for-Hong-Kong%E2%80%99s-Merchandise-Exports.htm [accessed 22 April 2010].

even smaller. In 2007, China's investment in ASEAN only made up around 1 percent of ASEAN's total FDI inflow, while ASEAN's investment in China was around 10 percent of the total FDI inflow to China in the same year. In 2008, China's investment in ASEAN was US$2.2 billion. In the first half of 2010 the amount of China's FDI in ASEAN countries was US$1.2 billion, an increase of 125.7 percent over the same period in the previous year.[19] This is a small fraction of China's outward FDI (see Figure 5.4 below). There is scope for substantial increase, which can serve as a clear indication of China's desire for greater economic integration with ASEAN.

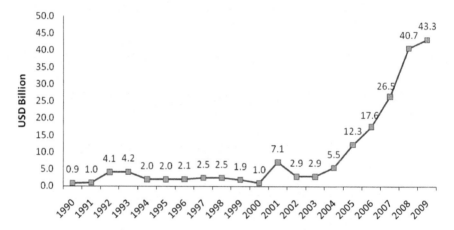

Figure 5.4.   China's outward FDI, 1999–2009.

Sources: China Statistical Yearbook 2009 and China Statistical Abstract 2010.

There is a need for China and ASEAN to encourage their SMEs or even state-owned enterprises (SOEs) to take advantage of the investment mechanisms in CAFTA to increase their investment across borders. For instance, China should take advantage of its growing overseas investment, brought about by its "going global" strategy, to not only increase its investment in the ASEAN region, but also to diversify the investment areas. Currently, the areas in which China's enterprises are investing are mostly energy, resource gathering and infrastructure. Other than facilitating greater integration between China and ASEAN, an increase in intra-regional investment can lead to the growth of the business community

---

19 "商务部: 今年上半年中国对美欧东盟投资倍增" [China's Ministry of Commerce: Chinese Investment in America, Europe and ASEAN Increased Multiple-Fold in First Half of the Year], 20 July 2010, http://www.un5.info/gncj/2010/0721/4012.html [accessed 22 July 2010].

in the CAFTA region as well as a better distribution of development. This will in turn contribute to the emergence of a broader-based middle class and the maintenance of a sustainable regional market.

Between them China and ASEAN cover a huge geographical area and a big economy with different levels of economic maturity, different resources and potential as well as different infrastructure needs. These aspects represent many opportunities for forward looking and bold cooperation. In most ASEAN countries, infrastructure is the first barrier to further development. There is a huge demand for transportation facilities for the Mekong River and other rivers, seaways, highways, railways, airways and bridges (such as the Java-Sumatra bridge). It would cost US$2 billion in 2007 prices to complete a railway across eight countries that will link Singapore to Kunming by 2015. An even bigger project is an initiative of the Asian Development Bank, the Greater Mekong Subregion project which started in 1992. It involves China, Myanmar, Laos, Thailand, Cambodia and Vietnam. The total investment in the GMS area is about US$14 billion between 1992 and 2011.

Another opportunity appears in the form of different labour costs in different regions or countries. For example, the average wage per month in Vietnam is about US$60, less than two thirds of the wage level in China's coastline cities. In Cambodia, Laos and Myanmar, the wage level is even lower. The wage level, land cost and environment protection have forced the labour-intensive industries to move out from the Pearl River Delta, Yangtze River Delta and other coastline areas. Being attracted to the opportunities offered by Vietnam, Cambodia, Laos and Myanmar, companies have relocated from China to the industrial parks set up in those countries.

The third opportunity comes from the differences in geographical conditions. The ASEAN nations are situated in tropical and sub-tropical regions with an annual rainfall of 1,500–2,000 mm and arable land of 153 million hectares, but only 65 percent of its resources are utilized. Thailand, Vietnam and Myanmar are world-renowned rice-producing countries. ASEAN also produces tropical produce, fruits, timbers and sea products. The primary industry makes up 12 percent of ASEAN's GDP, 13 percent of its exports and 45 percent of its labour force. If efficient modern agricultural enterprises can be established, then productivity will be greatly increased and a portion of its labour can be transferred to the manufacturing and service industries. China is rich with temperate produce and fruits but lacks water resources (especially in the north) and arable land. China can help ASEAN establish stable markets by importing tropical produce while exporting temperate produce and fruits.

Beneficial Nature of Trade

Trade is by its very nature an economic activity that is voluntary and mutually beneficial. Where two sides have the same industries producing similar goods, there is competition. Even though it may not be pleasant for the industries concerned, competition benefits consumers in terms of price and quality as well as choice. In the short term, governments are likely to be called upon to assist the weaker party to cope with the new situation.[20] Though there are concerns about the short-term difficulties, it is heartening to note that the prevalent attitude in ASEAN is to face up to the challenges and to emerge stronger in the long term: "Southeast Asian governments and firms have increasingly viewed China and its companies as formidable competitors for markets — in Southeast Asia itself and elsewhere — and for foreign direct investment ... Competition is basically good for economies and companies. In the face of fair Chinese competition, ASEAN countries have to strengthen the competitiveness of their own economies as well as their companies."[21]

Competition is the market mechanism favoured by those who believe strongly in the workings of a free market. But unbridled competition can also lead to unnecessary waste, and in adverse economic conditions, it may lead to friction. This can happen if one side chooses to use loopholes or resorts to non-tariff measures to protect its own industries. This is certainly not a distant possibility as it has already been suggested by Indonesia. The situation can lead to disputes, and it may severely test the dispute mechanism signed in 2004. This is an issue that should engage the attention of both ASEAN and China at the ministerial level.

It is therefore important for China that CAFTA demonstrate positive results for its ASEAN partners. For example, China unilaterally lowered the import tariffs on agricultural products and let its trading partners benefit from the "early harvest".

Investment in Production and Infrastructure

It would be useful for the CAFTA members to identify areas of cooperation that will deliver benefits to all concerned. China must also address the

---

[20] "Is China-ASEAN Free Trade Agreement — CAFTA Necessary to Renegotiate?", *Voice of Indonesia*, http://en.voi.co.id/voi-dignitorial/773-is-china-asean-free-trade-agreement-cafta-necessary-to-renegotiate.html [accessed 24 April 2010].
[21] Rodolfo C. Severino, "ASEAN-China Relations: Past, Present and Future", Paper presented at the Third China-Singapore Forum, Singapore, 17 April 2008.

concerns of trade deficits as experienced by some ASEAN members. It can increase the import of raw materials and agricultural produce (including seafood), and increase its direct investment especially in the area of natural resources.

There are win-win situations in investment in critical infrastructures and value-adding activities based on local human and natural resources. If done well, these will lead to employment, income growth, export and import growth, and higher standards of living. One simple example is the Indonesian province of Gorontalo with its fertile soils, poor physical infrastructure, and potential fishery industry.[22] There are no canneries to process the catch from the sea and no stable power supply. A lack of infrastructure can also be found in landlocked Laos where China will provide a long-term loan of US$4 billion to finance a railway network.[23]

There are challenges faced by China in investing in the ASEAN region. Because of historical reasons, ASEAN countries still hold some reservations about Chinese investment.[24] Moreover, China has not accumulated a vast amount of experience and built extensive business networks there. As the service centre of Southeast Asia, Singapore can play a useful role. With more than a few centuries of experience and accumulated skills in functioning as a financial centre and service centre, it can assist China with advice, networking and partnerships, thus creating win-win situations for all the parties involved.

Another point to note is that Chinese MNCs operating in the ASEAN region must not only abide by the best practices of their Western counterparts, but try to do even better. This is especially so in the area of exploitation of natural resources, which has a negative impact on the physical environment. The matter has to be handled well in order not to end up in a counterproductive situation. It has also been observed that Chinese firms have been occasionally enmeshed in cases of corruption in some ASEAN countries.[25]

---

[22] "Little-known Province Seeks Star Turn", *The Straits Times*, 23 April 2010.

[23] "China 'To Help Develop Laotian Rail Network'", *The Straits Times*, 1 May 2010.

[24] In the Cold War, China was on the side opposing America and was for decades seen by the old ASEAN-6 as keen on supporting communist movements in their countries. It was accused of having a hand in the 1966 coup in Indonesia.

[25] Rodolfo C. Severino, "ASEAN-China Relations: Past, Present and Future", Paper presented at the Third China-Singapore Forum, Singapore, 17 April 2008.

Coordination in Industrial, Fiscal and Monetary Policies

Trade is the most natural solution of wealth creation for two parties which have complementary products. Complementary economic activities can be a direct consequence of natural endowment, e.g. Malaysia and Indonesia exporting rubber and palm oil. But they can also be a result of history, technological capability, indigenous market size and FDI. This suggests that there is a role for industrial policy formulation, so that different countries and sub-regions can develop different areas of comparative prowess and competitive advantage. Here we can see clearly the benefits for ASEAN and China to strive towards coordination and mutual consultation in formulating their industrial policies. It is a kind of regionalism based on mutually beneficial division of "labour" without creating a situation favourable for monopolistic control of the market. In the long term, economic growth is driven by productivity. This is an important factor that should be considered when formulating industrial policies.

If we think beyond trade and consider the broader picture of economic relations, CAFTA members may do well to explore the issue of coordinating their fiscal and monetary policies. Of the two, monetary policy coordination is more important for the obvious reason that the exchange rate is often implicated in trade disputes.

Currently, Asian financial markets are more closely bound to the global market than to each other.[26] This has its historical reasons but the increasing volume of trade among the CAFTA members may provide the imperative for them to move towards closer integration of their financial sectors. Given the growing volume of trade and investment among the CAFTA members, especially between ASEAN nations and China, it does make sense to do business with the Chinese yuan as the currency. This lowers transaction costs in the form of uncertainty in the exchange rate.

Before concluding, we would like to add one last point. Unlike Europe, which has seen a retreat of nationalism, Asia must still cope with nationalism as a very powerful political force. And since nationalism is not going to fade away soon, regionalism has to bear this in mind. By its sheer size, CAFTA is a phenomenon worth studying, all the more so now that economic power is shifting from West to East. It is likely to yield interesting insights into FTA performance, regional cooperation and globalization.

---

[26] "Asia's Never-Closer Union", *The Economist*, 4 February 2010.

Chapter Six

The Flying Geese Model*

In the 1950s Japan embarked on an economic developmental path that came to be known as the flying geese model. The geopolitical milieu after World War II provided Japan with favourable conditions for rapid economic growth and industrialization. By the 1950s, many had noticed the success of the model and it was subsequently adopted by other East Asian countries. They too enjoyed decades of remarkable economic growth. An important element of the model is growth driven by exports to the USA and Europe. The bursting of the financial bubble in 1990 and Japan's subsequent response hold lessons for China.

As a result of the 2008 financial crisis, the traditional markets of the "geese" are shrinking. The new situation poses grave challenges to both the existing flying geese economies and the latecomer economies which wish to follow the model. East Asian countries are responding to the situation by broadening and deepening their existing economic linkages and developing new ones. This represents a continuation of East Asian regionalism in the wake of the 1997 financial crisis.

Introduction

It is widely accepted that the economic progress of Asia is one of the remarkable developments of the 20th century. At the time of independence several decades ago, many of the ex-colonies in Africa were on par with their Asian counterparts. But they are so very different today. "In 1960, South Korea's GDP matched Sudan's, and Taiwan's was about equal to that of the soon-to-be-independent Belgian Congo. By the 1990s, both Asian countries boasted living standards that rivaled those in the West.

---

*This chapter is an extended version of the paper by the second author "The 2008 Financial Crisis and the Flying Geese Model" which appears in *East Asia*, Vol. 27, No. 4 (2010), pp. 381–394.

More than 400 million people have been lifted out of poverty in China alone since the country began liberalizing its economy in 1980."[1]

An important element of the story is the flying geese model based on the Japanese experience. The model harks back to the end of World War II. The country had been devastated, and its industry lay in shambles. With few natural resources, Japan needed to import raw materials, but it lacked the foreign exchange necessary to do so. The answer presented itself in the form of using whatever industrial capacity still remaining to produce goods to sell to the world market and generate money to buy more advanced equipment and raw materials. The circumstances of its birth explain why the development path came into being without any real debate and without any generally accepted theoretical foundation.[2] Having said this, it is still to the credit of the Japanese elite that they managed to pull themselves together and embarked on what turned out to be a successful programme of economic reconstruction.

A defeated Japan had to follow the policies imposed by the US-led Allied forces which occupied the country until 28 April 1952. In the aftermath of the war, the supreme commander for the Allied powers exercised total control over Japan's foreign trade. Imports such as coal and oil were kept to a minimum.[3] "As a result, industrial production gradually declined, reaching a trough in January–February 1947 as inventories of basic materials ran out."[4] With the advent of the Cold War in 1947 after World War II, the aim of the occupation policy was to turn Japan into a bastion to contain Communism. Japan's fortune changed fundamentally with this new geopolitical situation. The task of economic reconstruction was made much easier with the outbreak of the Korean War in June 1950. The United States began to procure large quantities of goods and war materials to service its military operations in the Korean Peninsula. The USA acted as the main source of advanced technologies as well as the main market for its manufactured goods. And with the defense umbrella provided by the USA, Japan was in a position to commit its scarce resources to economic development.

---

[1]Brian P. Klein and Kenneth Neil Cukier, "Tamed Tigers, Distressed Dragon", *Foreign Affairs*, Vol. 88, Issue 4 (2009).

[2]R. Taggart Murphy, "Asia and the Meltdown of American Finance", *The Asia-Pacific Journal: Japan Focus*, 2008, http://japanfocus.org/-R_Taggart-Murphy/2931 [accessed on 12 December 2009].

[3]Juro Teranishi, *Evolution of the Economic System in Japan* (Cheltenham: Edward Elgar, 2005).

[4]Ibid., p. 172.

The postwar reconstruction imperatives and the global geopolitical environment were two key elements that explained the trajectory of Japan's economic development. This path was different from those which guided the development elsewhere in Asia then. There were two other models of development followed by their political leaders. One was the Marxist-Leninist model inspired by the Soviet Union. The other was the import substitution model favoured by non-communist, newly independent countries. In spite of the different political systems of these countries, the two models shared one similar goal. It was independence from imperialism which had oppressed them for so long. "Both called for state-directed capital accumulation and autarkic development, although the latter did allow for market mechanisms to function at the local level. Both boasted an extensive theoretical literature. In early postwar Asia, China would be the champion of the former, India of the latter."[5]

Leaving aside the obvious differences between the Marxist-Leninist model and the Japanese model, there are clear distinctions between the Japanese model and the import substitution model. Though both aimed at the development of domestic industries behind protectionist walls, they differed crucially in their stance towards the existing global economic order. India sought to eliminate its dependence on that order, while Japan chose to work within that order which it judged could serve its agenda best. Largely for geopolitical reasons, the United States was happy to accommodate Japan's drive to reinvent itself into an economic power in the shortest possible time and join the ranks of the non-communist developed nations.[6]

The Flying Geese Model

Very much in the tradition of the Meiji reform, Japan embarked on a trajectory of learning from the success of others. And it did so in a step-by-step fashion. It did not aim to create new industries. It focused on rapid accumulation of dollars so that it could buy the capital equipment it needed. It began by concentrating on industries like textiles and toy manufacturing, then moving on to shipping and steel, consumer electronics and consumer durables, machine tools and capital equipment. It is a story of industrial

---

[5]R. Taggart Murphy, "Asia and the Meltdown of American Finance", *The Asia-Pacific Journal: Japan Focus*, 2008, http://japanfocus.org/-R_Taggart-Murphy/2931 [accessed on 12 December 2009].
[6]Ibid.

upgrading, from low technology to high technology, from low-value-adding to high-value-adding activities. This pattern is captured metaphorically in the flying geese model.[7]

The original model as developed by Akamatsu is based on the pattern of economic development in one specific country, namely Japan.[8] The pattern consists of the following four stages:

Stage 1: Import of manufactured consumer goods.
Stage 2: Import substitution by importing capital equipment to produce these consumer goods.
Stage 3: Local industries export manufactured consumer goods.
Stage 4: Export of consumer goods declines while capital goods are exported.

Akamatsu extends his original model to describe the development of advanced and less-advanced countries. It is this multi-country model that is referred to as the flying geese model in the literature. The model describes the movement of industries in response to changes in factor prices. The initial stage of industrialization is marked by the setting up of labour-intensive industries to take advantage of the cheap and abundant supply of labour. As wages rise with rapid deployment of labour in these countries, investment in more capital-intensive activities takes place and there is a movement of labour-intensive industries to other countries.[9]

Japan's Experience and Its Appeal

At the level of business practice, the Japanese model is well known for its traditional practice of lifetime employment and seniority system. Under a business networking system known as *keiretsu*, companies that do a lot of business with each other hold equities in each other. At the core of

---

[7]Kename Akamatsu, "A Historical Pattern of Economic Growth in Developing Countries", *Journal of Developing Economies*, Vol. 1, No. 1 (1962), pp. 3–25.

Terutomo Ozawa, *Institutions, Industrial Upgrading, and Economic Performance in Japan — The 'Flying-Geese Paradigm of Catch-up Growth* (Northampton, MA: Edward Elgar Publishing, 2005).

Edith Terry, *How Asia Got Rich — Japan, China, and the Asian Miracle* (Armonk, New York: M.E. Sharp Publishing, 2002).

[8]Satoru Kumagai, "A Journey Through the Secret History of the Flying Geese Model", Institute of Development Economics Discussion Paper No. 158, Japan, 2008, http://www.grips.ac.jp/module/prsp/FGeese.htm_[accessed 28 January 2010].

[9]Ibid.

each group is a major bank which has great control over the companies in the *keiretsu*. As financier, it performs the function of monitoring the companies and acts as an emergency bailout entity. Besides acting as an organizational structure against hostile takeovers, it facilitates cooperation and information exchange among members of the group.

At the national level, there is close collaboration among business, government bureaucracy and the ruling political party. The state uses national resources to build the physical and social infrastructure to underpin rapid industrialization. While not denying the roles of free market and private enterprise, the state plays a strategic role in overcoming market imperfections, for example by favouring potentially competitive export-oriented industries with cheap credit. The approach has been captured in the concept of the developmental state, which implies a strong state.[10] Indeed, the developmental state is a distinct element of the modernization programme in East Asia. Even though it is not part of the formal definition of the flying geese model, the developmental state has been informally associated with it as an indispensable part of the East Asian model of economic growth.

The economic performance of Japan exceeded anyone's expectations. In 1955 the final elements of the postwar Japanese system were put into place. In 1969 its growth began to alter the global economic ecology which had fostered it. Within this period, Japan boasted the highest growth rates that had ever been recorded by any economy in human history. Between 1950 and 1973, the Japanese economy doubled in size every seven years, and it had achieved one of the highest standards of living in the world.[11] In the four decades until 1990, Japan stole the show in economic development. It had the world's highest saving rates and displayed an endless and amazing capacity to adapt to the latest industrial technologies. Japanese manufacturing became legendary. It coped well with the inflationary spurt in the wake of the OPEC oil price hikes in 1973.

After the 1970s, the technological strength of Japan's machinery and other manufacturing industries continued to prop up the economy, using exports as a lever. This strength was based on the innovative capacity of its technological firms.[12] Japan's emergence came as a tremendous

---

[10]Richard Appelbaum and Jeffrey Henderson (eds.), *States and Development in the Asian Pacific Rim* (Newbury Park, CA: Sage, 1992).

[11]Magnus Blomström, Byron Gangnes and Sumner la Croix (eds.), *Japan's New Economy* (Oxford: Oxford University Press, 2001).

[12]Hiroshi Yoshikawa, *Japan's Lost Decade* (Tokyo: The International House of Japan, 2001).

shock to many Western nations. Japanese firms entered and successfully competed in high-tech terrains which were previously the preserve of the US and European multinationals. The German camera industry had been the indisputable world leader, but it was almost wiped out by the Japanese competitor in just a decade from 1965 to 1975. Many US companies producing home appliances and machine tools were driven out of business. Until 1965 or so these industries were thought to be unrivalled.

Japan's prowess measured in terms of patents and productivity was the result of systematic and continuous investment in research and development (R&D). A study of the US Academy of Engineering published in 1987 observed that Japan was superior to the US in 25 of 34 critical technologies.[13] Based on its technological strength and financial power, Japan has managed to produce world-class companies like Mitsubishi, Sony, Toyota and Toshiba.

Given such a performance, the appeal of the path taken by Japan was too strong to ignore. By following the path, other East Asian countries have successfully embarked on the journey of economic growth and industrialization. In other words, the world is witnessing the implementation of the flying geese model. The hierarchy is headed by Japan, followed by the first tier of newly industrialized countries or NICs — Hong Kong, Singapore, South Korea and Taiwan. They are in turn followed by the second-tier NICs, namely Indonesia, Malaysia, the Philippines and Thailand. The third-tier countries are China, and more lately, the Indochina countries.

Pax Americana and Japan

It was mentioned earlier in the chapter that Japan has benefited economically from the defense umbrella provided by America. To be more concrete, "Pax Americana also provided Japan with liberal, stable environments for foreign trade, technology transfer, and a monetary system. Sufficient supplies of cheap energy and resources from abroad, easy access to advanced technologies of the West, and favorable conditions of the international payment system, all ingredients of Pax Americana, acted in concert and brought about the rapid economic growth experienced in Japan."[14] This geopolitical consideration

---

[13]National Academy of Engineering, *Strengthening U.S. Engineering through International Cooperation: Some Recommendations for Action* (Washington, DC: National Academy Press, 1987).
[14]Hiroshi Shibuya, Makoto Maruyama and Osamu Ito, "A Viewpoint to Analyze Japan's Social Economy and American Impacts", in Hiroshi Shibuya, Makoto Maruyama and Masamitsu Yasaka (eds.), *Japanese Economy and Society under Pax-Americana* (Tokyo: University of Tokyo Press, 2002), p. 4.

as manifested here applies to how the USA looks at other non-communist countries in the postwar global order.[15] Indeed, the USA, as the hegemon, had offered the developing countries its domestic markets for labour-intensive goods and services during the Cold War period. Even in the post-Cold War period, this policy continues, albeit for the economic logic followed by US transnational companies to outsource production to locations with the lowest cost possible in order to maintain profitability.

Viewed from the vantage point of history, the USA has played an important role in the development pattern of East Asian economies. It has been noted that "American policy in East Asia was to build up an integrated stable economic system with Japan acting as the region's 'economic workshop'. With the loss of Japan's traditional markets in China and Korea, the only alternative was to open new markets for Japanese goods in Southeast Asia. Washington promoted a triangular economic division of trade between the United States, Japan and Southeast Asia in which America would provide high technology and capital goods, Japan intermediate and consumer goods and Southeast Asia raw material and energy".[16]

Since 1968 until 2010, Japan moved up to become the second largest economy. As its economic power grows, Japan has been called upon by America to play its role in maintaining the US-led world order. In his speech on 15 August 1971, President Nixon conveyed this to America's trading partners: "Others should bear their fair share of the burden of defending freedom around the world and agree to exchange-rate changes that would enable major nations to compete as equals... There is no longer any need for the United States to compete with one hand tied behind her back."[17]

Japan was pressured to assume her share of maintaining the international economic system. The demand consisted of three points: realignment of exchange rates, opening up the domestic market, and assuming a larger share of the defense burden.[18] These three objectives have formed

---

[15]Terutomo Ozawa, "Asia's Labour-driven Economic Development, Flying-Geese Style: An Unprecedented Opportunity for the Poor to Rise?" World Institute for Development Economics Research, The United Nations University, 2005.

[16]W. R. Nester, *Japan and the Third World: Pattern, Power, Prospects* (London: Macmillan, 1992) p. 61.

[17]Alfred E. Eckes, Jr., *A Search for Solvency: Bretton Woods and the International Monetary System 1941–1971* (Austin: University of Texas Press, 1975), p. 263, quoted in Hiroshi Shibuya, Makoto Maruyama and Masamitsu Yasaka (2002).

[18]Robert Solomon, *The International Monetary System 1945–1976: An Insider's View* (New York: Harper & Row, 1977).

a cornerstone of US policy towards Japan until today. They provide a background for understanding the Plaza Accord of 1985.[19]

In other words, it was not just "one-way traffic". Japan has contributed time and again to the costs of maintaining the US-led economic and political world order.[20] A well-known example of Japan's contribution to the US military campaign is during the Gulf War in 1990–1991. Washington asked Tokyo to contribute to the campaign, arguing that "such actions would head off congressional criticism of Japanese free riding".[21] Japan contributed US$13 billion, a significant amount compared to the US$17 billion and US$16 billion contributed by Saudi Arabia and Kuwait respectively. The incremental costs (i.e. beyond the normal operating costs of the US military) of the war were estimated variously at US$70 billion, US$61 billion and under US$50 billion.[22]

Whenever the USA was in dire financial situation, it would call on Japan for assistance, and however grudgingly, Japan would oblige. "At crucial junctures in the past (the so-called Reagan Revolution of the early 1980s, for example, or the aftermath of the 1987 stock market crash), Japan had both the will and the ability to provide crucial assistance to Washington's recovery efforts. As America's principal external supplier of credit, Japan offered essentially unlimited, low-cost financing for the United States."[23] In a way, Japan has little choice. It depends on Washington for defense protection, as an export market and for maintaining a global order congenial to Japanese economic interests abroad.

The Asian Tigers and China

The stellar economic performance of Japan did not go unnoticed by its neighbours. Hong Kong, Singapore, South Korea and Taiwan enthusiastically adopted the model in the 1960s and 1970s. They in turn were joined by

---

[19] The goal of the Plaza Accord was to reduce the US dollar exchange rate in relation to the Japanese yen and German mark by intervening in currency markets. The Accord was signed by France, West Germany, Japan, the United States and the United Kingdom.

[20] Hitoshi Higuchi, "The Impact of Burden-Sharing on Japan: International Fiscal Policy Responses to the Decline of Pax Americana", in Hiroshi Shibuya, Makoto Maruyama and Masamitsu Yasaka (2002).

[21] Andrew Bennett *et al.* (eds.), *Friends in Need: Burden Sharing in the Persian Gulf War* (London: Macmillan, 1997), p. 147.

[22] Hitoshi Higuchi (2002).

[23] Tanaka Kiyoyasu, "Japan's Trade Collapse and Road to Recovery: Vertical Foreign Direct Investment the Key", *The Asia-Pacific Journal*, Vol. 20-4-09 (2009).

Indonesia, Malaysia, Thailand, Vietnam and China. This model of export-led growth was actively encouraged by the Western powers. In 1975, Robert McNamara, then president of the World Bank, urged Asian leaders to "turn their manufacturing enterprises away from the relatively small markets associated with import substitution towards the much larger opportunities flowing from export promotion".[24] More than three decades on, the effects have been remarkable.

These adopters of the flying geese model displayed both similarities with and differences from Japan. The Japanese developmental state model emphasizes the troika (ruling party, bureaucracy and business); other Asian countries on their own generally designed a state-led developmental model before the flying geese model was articulated. Through trial and error, the Japanese bureaucracy managed to use the state resources to intervene in an otherwise market economy in pursuit of economic modernization.[25] The policies formulated by the Ministry of International Trade and Industry have steered business to produce industrial expansion and economic growth. Japan is also relatively protectionist. Certain economic sectors do not welcome foreign participation. At the same time, it erects tariff walls or imposes quotas on certain imports deemed vital to its national culture, like rice. On the other hand, Hong Kong and Singapore are paragons of the free market and open economy. In South Korea, the state used naked power to suppress labour unrests and nurtured the development of giant family-owned industrial complexes known as *chaebol*.[26] In Taiwan, the state implemented land reform, which created a class of ex-landowners with capital.[27] These new capitalists invested their cash in subsequent industrialization. The Taiwanese government formulated a set of industrial policies to aim at export, heavy industry and chemicals, and later on electronics. The state was also able to use US foreign aid efficiently to develop its industrial base. Under state tutelage, Taiwanese industries moved from cheap, labour-intensive manufacturing into more capital-intensive and high-tech areas.

---

[24]Brian P. Klein and Kenneth Neil Cukier, "Tamed Tigers, Distressed Dragon", *Foreign Affairs*, Vol. 88, Issue 4 (2009).

[25]Chalmers Johnson, *MITI and the Japanese Miracle* (Stanford: Stanford University Press, 1982). Chalmers Johnson, *Japan: Who Governs?* — *The Rise of the Developmental State* (New York: W. W. Norton & Company, 1995).

[26]Alice H. Amsden, *Asia's Next Giant: South Korea and Late Industrialization* (Oxford: Oxford University Press, 1989). Ho-Joon Chang, "The Political Economy of Industrial Policy in Korea", *Cambridge Journal of Economics*, Vol. 17, No. 2 (1993).

[27]Robert Wade, *Economic Theory and the Role of Government in East Asian Industrialization* (Princeton: Princeton University Press, 1990).

The most remarkable is its semiconductor industry which ranks third or fourth in the world. In short, different members of the flying geese "club" exhibit unique features, partly shaped by culture and historical experiences and the political concerns of the political leadership.

Unlike Japan which has been lukewarm to foreign investment, other East Asian countries have thrown open their doors to multinational companies to set up factories, in order to provide employment, to facilitate the transfer of technology and management skills, and to earn foreign exchange. This approach is in line with the interests of the advanced industrial economies. To cope with rising costs of production, they relocate their production facilities to the emerging market economies to take advantage of cheap labour and land. The incentive to do so is even greater when the industries involved are polluting industries. The fierce competition posed by Japan ratchets up pressure on Western MNCs to relocate overseas.[28] The products are then exported back to the rich countries. The flying geese model has proved to offer a win-win situation to all the parties concerned. This is evident in the impressive economic development experienced by the Asian Tigers.

Perhaps the most eminent follower of the Japanese model is China. Since the economic reform initiated by Deng Xiaoping in 1978, China has gradually opened its doors to foreign investment. Most of the exported products from China are made by American, European, Japanese, Korean or Taiwanese companies, or produced under original equipment manufacturer agreements. This is in contrast to Japan, which places heavy restrictions on foreign investment, and exports to the West under their own brand names. This approach of China has helped to avert major trade frictions though there are relatively minor ones now and then. But it is not able to avoid the issue of employment. The voices of workers in America and Europe are very likely to grow louder in pressurizing their companies to move back.

From After the Cold War to the 1997 Asian Financial Crisis

East Asia has some seductive properties — political stability, an enormous pool of educated and hardworking workers, rich natural resources and

---

[28]Robert Brenner, *The Boom and the Bubble: The US in the World Economy* (London: Verso, 2003). Robert P. Brenner and Seong-jin Jeong, "Overproduction Not Financial Collapse is the Heart of the Crisis: The US, East Asia, and the World", *The Asia-Pacific Journal*, Vol. 6-1-09, 7 February 2009.

macroeconomic prudence. Since the mid-1980s, these countries have been chalking up impressive growth. Hong Kong, South Korea, Singapore and Taiwan are known as the four Little Dragons while Indonesia, Malaysia, the Philippines and Thailand are the four Asian Tigers. For example, from 1985 to 1995, Thailand might justifiably be seen as a model of an emergent economy. With an average GDP growth of 9.8 percent per annum it was the fastest growing country in the world during that period.[29]

Beginning in the early 1990s, soon after the end of the Cold War, global capital rushed into emerging markets in unprecedented quantities. Asia was the main destination of the deluge. The most fundamental change in the majority of East Asian economies in the 1990s was the dramatic increase in inflows of international capital. In 1996 alone, total net capital flows amounted to US$110 billion, compared to an annual average of less than US$17 billion a decade earlier.[30] The same year saw a new inflow of US$93 billion of private capital to Indonesia, Korea, Malaysia, the Philippines and Thailand.[31]

It was a period of free flow of private capital in huge quantities from the rich countries into East Asia. The motive was to have a share in the profits produced in these high-growth economies. However, such free-flowing capital was speculative in nature, and would leave at the first sign of what the investment community perceived to be trouble. In the midst of favourable reports of the economic performance of these countries, the Asian financial crisis broke out in July 1997 and caught many by surprise. Many commentaries, papers and books were published in its aftermath, attempting to understand and explain what went wrong. In the beginning, a popular view had it that state-guided industrialization had morphed into crony capitalism and corruption. Other factors were poor supervision of their financial sectors, especially when governments adopted a fixed exchange rate regime, etc. However, as time went on, such lines of argument lost some traction. For one thing, Hong Kong and Singapore could not be tarnished in any way with crony capitalism; moreover their financial sectors were well supervised. As for the rest of the countries, the reality of crony capitalism and industrial policies had been around for quite a long time. At

---

[29]Mihir Rakshit, *The East Asian Currency Crisis* (New Delhi: Oxford University Press, 2002), p. 44.

[30]Gregory Noble and John Ravenhill (eds.), *The Asian Financial Crisis and the Architecture of Global Finance* (Cambridge: Cambridge University Press, 2000).

[31]Cheol Eun and Bruce Resnick, *International Financial Management*, 5th edition (New York: McGraw Hill, 2009).

this point of writing, the most convincing factor appears to be concerted currency attacks by international speculators who suspected some real or apparent flaws in the economic fundamentals. The Asian financial crisis provides an empirical basis for many economists to argue for the merits of some form of currency control, a position endorsed by the International Monetary Fund (IMF) in early 2010. Perhaps we need some more years to really get to the root of the problem. For more detailed discussion of the causes of the crisis, interested readers may refer to the works cited in the footnote.[32]

It is interesting to note the different approaches adopted by the USA in regard to the 1997 Asian financial crisis and the 1994 Mexican peso crisis.[33] Washington acted promptly and decisively to contain the Mexican crisis and helped the economy to get back on track again. Uncle Sam obviously did not like the idea of a flood of workers and farmers made destitute by the crisis streaming across the border. The victim countries of the Asian financial crisis did not enjoy similar attention from the USA because they did not pose the same threat. There was also the factor of geopolitics after the fall of the Berlin Wall:

"Moreover, in the post-Cold War era, the US is less indulgent towards its allies because they are no longer needed to contain a Soviet Union

---

[32] For more on the Asian crisis, see, for example, the following books:

W. T. Woo, J. D. Sachs and K. Schwab (eds.), *The Asian Financial Crisis: Lessons for a Resilient Asia* (Cambridge, MA: MIT Press, 2000).

Gregory Noble and John Ravenhill (eds.), *The Asian Financial Crisis and the Architecture of Global Finance* (Cambridge: Cambridge University Press, 2000).

Gerald Tan, *The Asian Currency Crisis* (Singapore: Times Academic Press, 2000).

Mihir Rakshit, *The East Asian Currency Crisis* (New Delhi: Oxford University Press, 2002).

Pierre-Richard Agenor, Marcus Miller, David Vines and Axel Weber, *The Asian Financial Crisis — Causes, Contagion and Consequences* (Cambridge: Cambridge University Press, 1999).

[33] For more on the Mexican crisis, consult, for example, the following:

Thomas W. Slover, *Tequila Sunrise : Mexico Emerges from the Darkness of Financial Crisis* (London: London Institute of International Banking, Finance & Development Law, 1998).

U.S. General Accountability Office, *Mexico's Financial Crisis: Origins, Awareness, Assistance, and Initial Efforts to Recover,* http://www.gao.gov/archive/1996/gg96056.pdf [accessed on 29 November 2009].

G. A. Calvo and E. C. G. Mendoza, "Petty Crime and Cruel Punishment: Lessons from the Mexico Debacle", *American Economic Review,* Proceedings of the American Economic Association, Vol. 86, No. 2 (1996).

Francisco Gil-Diaz, "The Origin of Mexico's 1994 Financial Crisis", *The Cato Journal,* Vol. 17, No. 3 (1998).

that had collapsed... The US economic interests have increased in relative importance to security concerns and it was prepared to take advantage of the crisis in order to seek greater deregulation and market penetration into East Asian markets for the US corporate interests."[34]

Taking its cues from Washington, the IMF imposed tight monetary and austere fiscal policies as conditions for assisting those countries hit by the crisis. These policies hurt the poor and the innocent victims of the crisis. The IMF was criticized for protecting the interests of Western bankers at the expense of the borrower countries. The criticisms drew sympathetic agreement from some Western scholars and even bankers like George Soros. It has been noted that "the US government took advantage of the crisis to push long-sought trade goals".[35] The crisis was used as an opportunity for the USA to strengthen the grip of its hegemonic power: "With the end of Communism, the Asian tigers were seen in Washington as competitors, increasingly independent of US tutelage, hence the need to re-subordinate them... The IMF entry means the return of US hegemony and the decline of Asian capitalism as an independent and competitive pole."[36]

One cardinal lesson of the Asian financial crisis is that sound economic fundamentals are a poor guarantee against concerted attacks by a band of international speculators. Once those affected countries — either badly or not so badly — managed to emerge from the crisis, they decided that they would no longer live at the mercy of global financial speculators. They then resolved to build up their foreign reserves as a war chest to ward off global speculative attacks. And these huge foreign reserves are one factor in understanding the 2008 financial crisis.

Understanding the Flying Geese Model

The model has a chequered history. It was used as part of Japanese propaganda during World War II to lend legitimacy to the Greater Asia Co-Prosperity Sphere, and this continued to tarnish the image of the model

---

[34] Lam Peng Er, "The Asian Financial Crisis and Its Impact on Regional Order: Opening Pandora's Box", *The Journal of Pacific Asia*, Vol. 6 (2000), pp. 57–80.

[35] Gregory W. Noble and John Ravenhill, "Causes and Consequences of the Asian Financial Crisis", p. 22, in Gregory W. Noble and John Ravenhill (2000).

[36] Quoted on p. 451 in Paul Burkett and Martin Hart-Landsberg, "East Asia and the Crisis of Development Theory", *Journal of Contemporary Asia*, Vol. 28, No. 4 (1998), pp. 435–456.

for some time after the war.[37] With the rapid growth of the Japanese economy in the 1960s till the 1980s, the model began to attract more favourable and wider attention. It gained rapid and wide popularity after it was presented by former Japanese Foreign Minister Saburo Okita to the world at a conference in Seoul in 1985.[38]

One interpretation of the flying geese model is based on its use by Japanese militarism in World War II. Japan would always remain at the top, i.e. it would be impossible for other countries to adopt the Japanese model, unless they accepted Japanese leadership.[39] It has some points of affinity with the idea of international division of labour used to justify the exploitation of colonies as suppliers of raw materials to their imperial masters.

Another interpretation is to consider the possibility that the pattern of the geese flight can change. In other words, the model can be understood to mean one of asymmetrical catch-up, as the latecomers absorb knowledge from the leader. This seems to reflect the emerging situation in East Asia. As a very advanced industrial economy, Japan is finding it increasingly difficult to keep up its former pace of innovation and technological advancement. Together with its social problem of ageing and cultural policy of not accepting waves of immigration, its economy has been stuck in recession since the bursting of the bubble in 1990. Meanwhile, NICs like South Korea are steaming ahead and China is rapidly catching up on all fronts. And much of the good news in the Japanese economic picture comes from its trade with China. The same might be said for the economies of Taiwan and Indonesia. We must remain open to the idea of a modified or revised form of the model.

Another point to bear in mind in trying to understand the model is that the various East Asian countries have their own historical background, socio-political concerns, cultures, institutions and economic agendas. Even though the differences may not be huge in certain aspects, they do have an impact on the actual adoption of the Japanese experience. For example, the Japanese-style general trading companies enjoy varying degrees of success in the different countries. Its adoption in South Korea was a success story,

---

[37]Shigehisa Kasahara, "The Flying Geese Paradigm: A Critical Study of Its Application to East Asian Regional Development", UNCTAD Discussion Paper No. 169, United Nations Conference on Trade and Development, Geneva.

[38]Saburo Okita, "Special Presentation: Prospect of Pacific Economics", the Fourth Pacific Economic Cooperation Conference, 28 April to 1 May 1985, Korea Development Institute, Seoul.

[39]This was pointed out by an anonymous reviewer.

expanding exports while assembling business conglomerates, but somehow Taiwan's adoption was a failure.[40]

During the heyday of the model, it became a prescriptive tool employed by the Japanese bureaucrats in their dealings with other East Asian countries. What Japan used to do had to be followed by the Asian NICs, and what the Asian NICs used to do had to be followed by the ASEAN countries.[41]

Because of the geopolitical background, we must be cautious in drawing parallels between Japan and China in discussing the flying geese model. Japan is a close ally of America in East Asia. In exchange for military protection provided by the USA and the American market for Japanese goods, Japan is willing to open its wallet for the privileges. For several decades, the relationship has proved to be very productive for both sides as a whole.

The same certainly cannot be said of Beijing's relationship with Washington. Due to ideological differences and issues like Taiwan and Tibet, America will not treat China as a second Japan. Neither will China be willing to behave like Japan in regard to its relationship with America. China is not going to pay for part of American military expenses in maintaining the present world order. Some Washington officials may argue that America has been spending tremendous resources to maintain Pax Americana by suppressing piracy and fighting terrorism, and China is behaving like a free rider. But this view is not shared by Beijing officials.

That does not mean that the two powers will inevitably clash. Many big US corporations have a vested interest in the well-being of China. In terms of trade and investment, China is more open than Japan. Boeing is a big supplier of China's airlines. Wal-Mart depends on China to supply cheap consumer products. Many American companies have manufacturing facilities in China. In fact, most of the products exported to America are made by American companies based in China. After China's accession to

---

[40]R. F. Doner, "Japanese Foreign Investment and the Creation of a Pacific Asian Region", in J. A. Frankel and M. Kahler (eds.), *Regionalism and Rivalry: Japan and the United States in Pacific Asia* (Chicago: University of Chicago Press, 1993).

Shigehisa Kasahara, "The Flying Geese Paradigm: A Critical Study of Its Application to East Asian Regional Development", UNCTAD Discussion Paper No. 169, United Nations Conference on Trade and Development, Geneva.

[41]M. Bernard and J. Ravenhill, "Beyond Product Cycles and Flying Geese: Regionalization, Hierarchy, and the Industrialization of East Asia", *World Politics,* Vol. 47 (1995), pp. 171–209.

the World Trade Organization in 2001, Western transnational companies (TNCs) invested heavily in China — both to make good use of the cheap labour and to gain a foothold in the vast market. Unlike investment from overseas Chinese before this, these TNCs brought special benefits to China in the form of technological transfer. China is shrewd enough to use its market size to negotiate deals which include transfer of high technology, for example the deals with Airbus to produce planes in China, and semiconductor production plants.[42] The relationship between America and China is complex and has to be handled with care, wisdom and commitment to mutual interests. As noted by a lead article in an issue of *The Economist*: "... America and China are not just rivals for global influence, they are also mutually dependent economies with everything to gain from co-operation."[43]

Two Additional Points for China to Note

There are two other features of Japan's experience that China should take note of. One is the formation of world-class transnational companies. The other is the long drawn-out recession after the bursting of the bubble in 1990.

First, the formation of competitive transnational companies. In the midst of the Japanese recession, it is easy to forget that by the 1970s — three decades after its disastrous defeat in World War II — Japan could boast of an impressive list of world-class transnational companies. Names like Mitsubishi, Nomura, Sumitomo and Toyota are well known in the global business landscape. Transnational companies are a business species best suited to exploit the conditions of globalization. They treat the world as their marketplace to sell their products, as their source of finance, talents and production materials. To China's credit, it has Sinopec, China National Petroleum, Industrial and Commercial Bank of China, Haier and ZTE. But most of these are resource-based corporations owned and controlled by the Chinese state. In contrast with Japan, very few of the Chinese transnational companies are privately owned and operate on the world stage like their Japanese counterparts. In this aspect, South Korea has done very well, while it is a weak spot of the Chinese economy.

---

[42]Michael Heng Siam-Heng, "China's Semiconductor Industry — Opportunities and Challenges", in E. Thomson and J. Sigurdson (eds.), *China's Science and Technology Sector and the Forces of Globalisation* (Singapore, World Scientific, 2008), pp. 173–189.
[43] "Facing Up to China", *The Economist*, 6 February 2010, p. 9.

Where market and individual initiatives should be the main driving force in creating and nurturing competitive Chinese transnational firms, the state can and should give the whole process a helping hand. One way to do so is by way of industrial policy. Among other things, it will be in China's interests to nurture companies active in the following areas: manufacturing, engineering, information technology, banking and finance, biotechnology and agriculture, medicine and healthcare, trading, communication and transport, mass media and publishing. Together they cover areas that are of core interest to a big country. Notice that industries like cosmetics and tourism are not included. Though they can be of business interest in the sense of money making, they are not essential for national defense and a solid foundation for economic development.

Second, the lesson of Japan's "lost decade". Ever since Japan's miracle ground to a halt in 1990, the country has found it immensely difficult to return to the glorious days of the pre-1990 period. Various reasons for the slowdown have been proposed. A well-known one is that the Japanese banks were not restructured quickly and deeply enough to provide funds to the needy individual and business borrowers. Another is the demographic factor. The birthrate has been falling for years below the necessary replacement rate. Coupled with people living longer, Japan has a decreasing population supporting an increasing retired ageing population. Yet another is the balance sheet recession proposed by Richard Koo.[44] By that, Koo means the Japanese businesses are so heavily in debt that even after the businesses make profits, they must use their profits to repay the debts rather than investing in new equipment and recruitment. With businesses operating in low gear, the economy has been kept afloat by a series of government spending programmes and years of very low interest rates. Elsewhere we have also discussed the importance of innovation, technological breakthroughs and the need for educational reform as measures to deal with the challenges.[45]

Though there is no final word on the set of critical factors that account for the state of Japan's economy, China can take away some useful lessons. Number one is the need for technological innovation and breakthroughs, a key factor in promoting economic growth and development. Number two is

---

[44]Richard C. Koo, *The Holy Grail of Macroeconomics*, revised and updated edition (Singapore: John Wiley, 2009).
[45]Michael Heng Siam-Heng, *The Great Recession: History, Ideology, Hubris and Nemesis* (Singapore: World Scientific, 2010).

the danger of blowing up the real estate bubble as a way to pump up GDP figures, a point too obvious to labour on after the subprime debacle in the USA. Number three is the problems associated with an ageing population. With its one-child policy in operation for three decades, China is bound to be confronted with the demographic "deficits" in the fullness of time. As a society becomes richer, there is a trend to have small families, even to the point of going below the replacement rate. In this sense, there is no reason for other countries to feel that they are immune from Japan's problems. In other words, all the East Asian countries which are on the road to becoming richer will have to watch and learn from how Japan manages to deal with its problems.

Implications of the 2008 Financial Crisis

As a result of the success of the flying geese model, an interesting pattern has appeared in global trade. Japan and emerging economies rely on an export-oriented strategy to drive their economic growth. Using part of their export earnings, they build up substantial foreign reserves as a defensive measure against speculative attacks. The money is held in US dollars, which is used by America to finance public and private consumption. Over the years, this builds up a global imbalance in the form of ballooning US trade deficits and fiscal deficits. With the outbreak of the financial crisis in September 2008, these twin deficits have featured prominently in discussions on the economic outlook for America.

An outcome of the 2008 financial crisis is that the USA is increasing its pressure on East Asian countries (notably China) to reduce their bilateral trade surplus with it. This poses a great challenge for the regional economies to bring about a situation more acceptable to Uncle Sam. The impact on the trade pattern is likely to be more regional trade within East Asia.

In the short term, Western consumers are working hard to repair their household balance sheets by cutting down consumption: "Exports from East Asian countries to their traditional market in the West have plunged across the board, and they are unlikely to recover soon. The West's great consumption binge is unlikely to return anytime soon, leading to excess industrial capacity, financial difficulties for businesses, and rising unemployment throughout Asia."[46]

---

[46]Brian P. Klein and Kenneth Neil Cukier, "Tamed Tigers, Distressed Dragon", *Foreign Affairs*, Vol. 88, Issue 4 (2009).

Two points need highlighting, namely the dwindling market in the West, and excess industrial capacity. The implication is that the flying geese model in the present form is not sustainable, and China may well be the last member to have successfully joined the flight. China has been known as the workshop of the world for some time. Unless there is a huge market for consumer goods appearing suddenly somewhere, it is difficult to see how another country can repeat China's export experience.

What does it mean for other countries which want to modernize and industrialize? Before the outbreak of the crisis, these questions could be pushed backstage. After all, the West seemed to exhibit an inexhaustible appetite and capacity in absorbing the manufactured goods. As long as the going was good, problems arising from the global financial imbalance could only command the attention of a tiny group of people. The crisis has now brought the question to the agenda of the existing members of the flying geese. How should East Asian countries adjust their economic policies to cope with the new situation?

One evident answer is provided by the stimulus policy adopted by China and other countries. As much has been written on this, this chapter will not dwell on it, except to point out that the allocation for education and healthcare is far too small. The economic recession justifies running fiscal deficits to pump-prime the economy and governments would do well to make good use of the opportunity to invest in social infrastructure and institute social safety nets. It has been observed that in the age of globalization, the quality of state expenditure as part of Keynesian stimuli is very important.[47]

Running fiscal deficits weakens the financial position of a country, and may attract speculative attacks on its currency. As a safeguard, emerging economies can follow the policy of Chile, China and India to restrict free currency flow. Perhaps this should be adopted as a policy during normal times too. This reduces considerably the need to keep huge foreign reserves as a defense against currency speculators, and the money can be more profitably used for socially useful and economically productive investment. Besides social spending, a good way to spend some of the money is to buy appropriately advanced technologies from the West. Not only are they generally cheaper in times of recession, the move will also reduce the trade

---

[47]Richard C. Koo, *The Holy Grail of Macroeconomics*, revised and updated edition (Singapore: John Wiley, 2009).

deficits of countries like the USA and Great Britain. This will help to redress the global imbalances.

Finally, East Asian countries should broaden and deepen the existing economic linkages among themselves and develop new ones. This follows the response to East Asian regionalism after the 1997 Asian financial crisis. Until the crisis, even though the tide of regionalism was sweeping across the region, it was not firmly established. The Asian crisis provided the occasion for the affected countries to work towards closer Asian integration in trade, investment, production and consumption. The current global recession has given them yet another push towards deeper and tighter regional integration. This will add to the various initiatives to build physical infrastructures such as roads, railways and ports.[48] An important milestone of this trend is the recent implementation of the China-ASEAN Free Trade Agreement,[49] though many challenges still lie ahead.

Most crucial of all is the imperative to cooperate in evolving complementary industrial policies, which will form the solid basis for trade and economic integration. Should East Asia fail in this project, they have only themselves to blame.

Concluding Remarks

The flying geese model has proved its merits in the form of the remarkable economic performance of East Asia. Even though it failed to provide conceptual pointers for Japan to get out of its "lost decades" after the bursting of the bubble in 1990, it has continued to guide the economic trajectory of other East Asian countries. One useful insight is that the state can play an effective role in economic development through various forms of intervention. This goes against the fundamental tenets of a canonical liberal market economy.

During the 1997 Asian financial crisis, it was suggested that the solution lay in the transfer of technology and production from advanced countries to the poorest countries.[50] It has been observed that by following this model, whether consciously or otherwise, East Asia has recovered.[51] In the

---

[48] Asian Development Bank, *Infrastructure for a Seamless Asia* (Manila: ADB, 2009).

[49] See an earlier chapter in this volume on CAFTA.

[50] Steven Radelet and Jeffrey Sachs, "Asia's Reemergence", *Foreign Affairs*, Vol. 76 (1997), pp. 44–59.

[51] Kiyoshi Kojima, "The "Flying Geese" Model of Asian Economic Development: Origin, Theoretical Extensions and Regional Policy Implications", *Journal of Asian Economics*, Vol. 11 (2000), pp. 365–401.

aftermath of the 2008 global financial crisis, economists and policy makers have again seen the flying geese model as a means to energize the regional markets and develop new hubs of production networks. This is likely to result in more intraregional trade and to help address the negative impacts of the crisis. The revival of the model this time round may see a new wave of countries involved. Whereas Japan used to be the lead driver in the past, the new schema will perhaps have China and South Korea at the helm, with the lower-income Asian countries following.[52]

As is evident from its genesis, the flying geese model was developed as a pragmatic response to the pressing needs of the time, a sort of model based on situational logic rather than any grand and coherent economic theory. This happens to be a feature of the financial policies of China and India. The two countries have gone against the strong current of financial liberalization which started in earnest in the mid-1980s. Though their financial policies are not seen as an integral part of the flying geese model, they may be seen as following the spirit of the model. If Asian countries follow such a spirit in facing the challenges of the current global recession, they may be able to provide valuable solutions both for themselves and for the rest of the world.

---

[52] "The Flying Geese Model of Regional Development", *Economic Issue of the Day*, Vol. X, No. 1 (2010), Philippine Institute for Development Studies, http://dirp4.pids.gov.ph/ris/eid/pidseid1001.pdf [accessed 21 June 2010].

Chapter Seven

Reflections on Developmental Models

One upshot of the 2008 financial crisis and the subsequent recession in the West is a renewed interest in economic developmental models. In news reports and commentaries, two other models very often come into the picture, namely the Washington Consensus and the Beijing Consensus. This chapter will dwell on the key points of these two models and explain why the Beijing Consensus has enjoyed lukewarm reception among Chinese policy makers and intellectuals. Unlike a model designed for natural sciences applications, an economic model needs to consider the context of its application.

Looking ahead, China may find it useful to study the experiences of the Nordic countries. They are able to combine social security with economic dynamism, have low income disparity, low crime rates, high standards of living, good healthcare and are concerned about the environment.

The Washington Consensus

We begin with the Washington Consensus for two reasons. First, the word "consensus" has been popularized by it and has become a catchy term used to describe a useful experience of socio-economic development.[1] Second, debates on economic growth in the developing countries have frequently made reference to the Consensus. In his piece expounding the original version of the Washington Consensus, John Williamson attempted to draw out the positive experience in Latin America up to 1989 that would meet the approval of official Washington (US politicians and senior White House officials and the Federal Reserve Board, the World Bank and the International Monetary Fund). The experience is summarized by Williamson as macroeconomic stability, domestic liberalization and

---

[1] See its usage in the Beijing Consensus, Copenhagen Consensus, Mumbai Consensus and Seoul Consensus.

international openness, or more popularly as a list of ten points:

1. Fiscal discipline.
2. A redirection of public expenditure priorities from things like indiscriminate subsidies to basic health, education and infrastructure.
3. Tax reform by constructing a tax system that would combine a broad tax base with moderate marginal tax rates.
4. Liberalizing interest rates.
5. A competitive exchange rate.[2]
6. Trade liberalization.
7. Liberalization of inward foreign direct investment.
8. Privatization.
9. Deregulation.
10. Property rights.

Though Williamson said that the Consensus was in principle historically and geographically specific, he also claimed that "in practice there would probably not have been a lot of difference if I had undertaken a similar exercise for Africa or Asia, and that still seemed to be the case when I revisited the topic (with regard to Latin America) in 1996".[3] Such ambiguity is unfortunate, for readers would believe that the Consensus was meant to apply to the developing countries in Asia and Africa as well.

When its critics looked at the experiences of economic growth in East Asia, they had much to disagree with the Consensus. Privatization, deregulation and financial liberalization were not supported by most of the East Asian countries. The success stories of East Asia were those of state intervention, industrial policies, and limited financial liberalization and capital control. South Korea even restricted inward foreign direct investment while Japan exercised trade protectionism. In view of the ideological climate in Washington in the 1980s, it is not surprising that some critics have called the Washington Consensus a product of neoliberalism[4]

---

[2]Williamson defines it as one that is not overvalued, but not as one that is undervalued. Source: John Williamson, "The Choice of Exchange Rate Regime: The Relevance of International Experience to China's Decision", Keynote speech at a conference on exchange rates organized by the Central University of Finance and Economics in Beijing on 7 September 2004, p. 6, http://www.iie.com/publications/papers/williamson0904.pdf [accessed 22 November 2010].
[3]John Williamson, "What Should the World Bank Think about the Washington Consensus", *The World Bank Research Observer*, Vol. 15, No. 2 (2000), pp. 251, 254–5.
[4]Joseph E. Stiglitz, *Globalization and its Discontents* (New York: Norton, 2002).

or market fundamentalism.[5] A kinder view is to note that because freedom, liberty and equality are values championed by the USA, the Washington Consensus is its ideological model of economic development.

What about those who keep an open mind and try to extract what is useful from the Consensus in their actual practice in economic development? One such person is Arnold Harberger. To him, the Washington Consensus can be interpreted as "a pragmatic distillation derived from some four decades of postwar experience in a host of developing countries".[6] He cautioned against seeing it as a cookie-cutter approach to development policy, derived from a blind application of neoclassical economics to the problems of the developing countries. In other words, it is "something quite different from a faithful reflection of modern neoclassical economics in the medium of economic policy".[7] In fact, it has been quite tolerant of moderate fiscal deficits, moderate rates of inflation, moderate ranges of import tariffs and moderate tax rates generally. On the question of privatization, Harberger insisted on meticulous preparation by the government before selling off state-owned companies, as meticulously as General Electric would do in the process of selling off a daughter company. Similarly, he readily admitted that "in probably more than half of the 'growth miracle' episodes of recent decades, some form of capital or exchange control was in place".[8]

Since the launch of its reform in 1978, China has been learning from others' experience. It is inconceivable that the policy makers and government economists in China have not studied the Washington Consensus.[9] Like Harberger, they have not blindly followed it. Of the three principles of macroeconomic stability, domestic liberalization and international openness propounded by Williamson, China is certainly in favour of

---

[5] George Soros, *The Crisis of Global Capitalism* (New York: Public Affairs, 1998).

[6] Arnold C. Harberger, "The View from the Trenches: Development Processes and Policies as Seen by a Working Professional", in Gerald M. Meier and Joseph E. Stiglitz (eds.), *Frontiers of Development Economics — the Future in Perspective* (New York: Oxford University Press, 2000), p. 549.

[7] Ibid., p. 550.

[8] Ibid., p. 551.

[9] Chinese publications discussing Chinese economic development often devote some space to dwell on the concept of the Washington Consensus. See, for example, the following: Ren Jiantao, "Corrected State Philosophy and the Chinese Model", Working Paper No. 85, East Asian Institute, National University of Singapore, 2010. 黄平, 崔之元 (主编), 中国与全球化: 华盛顿共识还是北京共识 (北京: 社会科学文献出版社, 2005). (Huang Ping and Cui Zi Yuan (eds.), *China and Globalization* (Beijing: Social Sciences Academic Press, 2005).)

macroeconomic stability and international openness. Bearing this in mind, it is not wrong to say that China's economic policies show both similarities and differences when compared with the Washington Consensus. Their similarities suggest that China's policies reveal a very sophisticated learning from the Washington Consensus. Their differences suggest that China has charted an independent path and its experience is captured in the Beijing Consensus.

The Beijing Consensus

By any standards, the record of China's economic development since the economic reform promulgated in 1978 is remarkable. As many volumes have been devoted to describing the achievements, they will not be repeated here.[10] What then are the secrets of the Chinese success and how can the rest of the developing countries learn from China's experience? At the level of practice, China certainly has formulated a set of policies that deviate somewhat from the list of ten points produced by Williamson. This can easily lead to the conclusion that China's experience represents a powerful case against the Washington Consensus. This is the view taken by a number of eminent economists, e.g. Joseph Stiglitz and Dani Rodrik.[11]

Based on his observations while working in China, Joshua Cooper Ramo found that China's economic development differed from the Washington Consensus on a few significant points. China follows the concept of the developmental state, where the country's economic development is very much dependent on the state. State-owned enterprises play dominant roles in oil exploration, refinery and distribution, banks, communications and transport, etc. By virtue of its design and implementation of industrial policies, the state has a big say in determining the direction of economic development. Moreover, it has control over capital flows and sets exchange rates. Ramo finds these significant conceptual departures from the Washington Consensus. In other words, he feels that China offers an alternative

---

[10]See, for example, the following: 林毅夫, 蔡昉, 李周, 中国的奇迹: 发展战略和经济改革 (上海: 三联书店, 1999). (Lin Yifu, Cai Fang and Li Zhou, *The Chinese Miracle: Development Strategy and Economic Reform* (Shanghai: Sanlian Bookstore, 1999).) John Wong and Wei Liu, *China's Surging Economy: Adjusting for More Balanced Development* (Singapore: World Scientific, 2007). 唐晋 (主编), 大国策: 经济模式 (北京: 人民出版社, 2009). (Tang Jin (ed.), *Big Power Strategy: Economic Models* (Beijing: Renmin Publishing House, 2009).)

[11]Huang Ping and Cui Zi Yuan (2005).

model, which he calls the Beijing Consensus.[12] This new consensus has three key features:

1. Innovation and constant experimentation.
2. Rejection of GDP growth above all, in favour of sustainability and equality.
3. Self-determination (i.e. beating an independent path in all major issues).

Just like the Washington Consensus, the Beijing Consensus has its critics. They are not persuaded that China rejects GDP growth in favour of sustainability and equality. The point is quite evident, given the widespread pollution and growing income disparity. China's economic architects have not generated groundbreaking fresh ideas either. Scott Kennedy observes the following:

"Since China's reality does not approach the WC [Washington Consensus] ideal, Ramo hails the country's uniqueness. However, if he applied a more nuanced comparative lens, he would discover that China's policies and trajectory share similarities and differences with a wide range of countries, including those with more liberal capitalist governance regimes and those with developmental states. This is in part because *the intellectual source for most of China's economic reforms has been the experiences of other countries, and China's experts and officials have closely examined and borrowed from elsewhere* [emphasis added]."[13]

It is thus not surprising that the Beijing Consensus has generally failed to find resonance with Chinese intellectuals and government officials, for they are aware of the history. The journey of economic reform in China started in late 1978 when the Third Plenary Session of the 11th CPC Central Committee decided to close the chapter of the Great Proletarian Cultural Revolution and to embark on a programme of economic modernization. The session was a turning point in the history of both the Party and the country.[14]

The following six years saw the country shrugging off the shackles of the planned economy and exploring a workable new system. It started

---

[12] Joshua Cooper Ramo, "The Beijing Consensus" (2004), reprinted in Huang Ping and Cui Zi Yuan (2005).

[13] Scott Kennedy, "The Myth of the Beijing Consensus", http://www.indiana.edu/~rccpb/Myth%20Paper%20May%2008.pdf [accessed 29 November 2010].

[14] "Milestones of Reform: 30 Years of 3rd Plenums", http://www.china.org.cn/government/central_government/2008-10/08/content_16584646.htm [accessed 20 January 2011].

with a household land-contracting system. While fulfilling the state quota, peasants could plant cash crops and keep animals like chickens and pigs. At the same time, industrial and commercial enterprises (all state-owned) in the cities experimented with greater autonomy in decision-making. Another bold step was taken when China set up free trade zones in Shenzhen, a southern coastal fishing village. It was a clear sign of China learning from other developing countries.

In 1984, it was stated for the first time that China's socialist economy was not a planned economy per se, but a planned commodity economy based on public ownership. Given the ideological straitjacket in the pre-reform years, it was a major ideological breakthrough for the CPC. It also marked the spreading of reforms from rural areas to the cities and to the whole economy.

After the end of the Cold War, the free market ideology rose to commanding heights. The subsequent reform instituted by Moscow was very much in line with the neoliberal recommendations originating from the USA. But the reform project ended up as a fiasco. Though China avoided the Russian mistake, it too drew ideological inspiration from neoliberal thinking in 1992.[15] This was in the aftermath of the famous inspection tour by China's de facto leader Deng Xiaoping of the coastal free trade zones in the south. Impressed by what he saw, he urged the Chinese people to follow the example of the free trade zones, to embrace the market economy and to get rich. The call was a well-considered response to the problems facing the leadership after the Tiananmen Square protests in June 1989. China had to speed up the economic reform in order to enlarge the economic cake and provide employment in order to preempt future social unrest. "The central task is to develop the economy and the rest will take care itself." This creed is very much in line with neoliberal thinking. Chinese neoliberal scholars and policy makers are on the same wavelength as their peers in the Western world, especially the United States. They stress the economic benefits of unfettered markets, privatization of state enterprises and a minimalist state role. Chinese neoliberals have enthusiastically embraced China's integration with the world economy, especially after its accession to the World Trade Organization in 2001.

The significance of the Beijing Consensus may lie more in its political wisdom than its original economic thinking. Policies like fiscal responsibility,

---

[15]Bo Zhiyue and Chen Gang, "Financial Crisis Enhances Stand of China's New Left", *EAI Bulletin*, Vol. 11, No. 1 (2009).

high savings and high investment are mainstream economic advice found in the pages of economic textbooks. What sets China apart from many other developing countries is its ability to see that the policies are carried out. It has been argued that "that the term [Beijing Consensus] derives its meaning and appeal not from some coherent economic or political position but from its suggestion of a pole in the global political economy which can serve as a gathering place for those who are opposed to Washington imperialism".[16] Many developing countries are impressed by China's economic growth, and "at the same time, chafe at the paternalism and stipulations that come with American advice and aid. No one seems to be comfortable with a world with just one superpower".[17]

From such a perspective, Ramo's enthusiasm is not misplaced. For one thing, he and many other observers (his critics included) concur that China's economic development was and still is based on open-mindedness and learning from the experiences of others while keeping close to the concrete social, political and historical conditions of China. Ramo writes, "The Beijing Consensus adheres closely to Deng Xiaoping's idea of groping for rocks to cross the river."[18] In view of such learning, it is only sensible for China to pick up tips from both the positive and negative lessons from Latin America and therefore the Washington Consensus. When Beijing exercises fiscal discipline, whether it does so from its own experience or as an upshot of learning from others is less important.

Here, it is useful to recognize the simple fact that China still faces a host of teething problems. China is in the midst of dealing with economic growth, modernization, unemployment, pollution, corruption and housing problems while preserving social stability and national integrity. Until it is clearer how these herculean tasks can be solved, it may be better to talk about a model in formation. Such a still unformed model has been expressed by the Chinese public intellectual Li Zehou. He is in favour of a Chinese model, one that is different from the socialism of the past and yet different

---

[16] Arif Dirlik, "Beijing Consensus: Beijing "Gongshi." Who Recognizes Whom and to What End?", Globalization and Autonomy Online Compendium, http://www.global-autonomy.ca/global1/position.jsp?index=PP_Dirlik_BeijingConsensus.xml [accessed 2 December 2010].

[17] "Is There a Beijing Consensus?", International Political Economy Zone, 21 February 2007, http://ipezone.blogspot.com/2007/02/is-there-beijing-consensus.html [accessed 2 December 2010].

[18] Joshua Cooper Ramo, "The Beijing Consensus" (2004), reprinted in Huang Ping and Cui Zi Yuan (2005).

from capitalism. It is a new model that must be able to make contributions to humankind. But this "third path" has not yet taken shape.[19]

Back to the Realm of Political Economy

As noted in the previous chapter, China has learned a lot from Japan and it is generally seen to be a third-tier goose in the flying geese formation of East Asian economic emergence. This point has an important theoretical implication, namely the linkage between economic growth and political system.

Japan is generally seen as a democracy and not an authoritarian state. Its general election is free and fair. There is freedom of the mass media and other freedoms associated with democracy. The civil service, the police and the small armed forces are generally perceived to be free from corruption. Japan's experience suggests that economic development is linked to a democratic political system. Either the economic development is a product of the democratic political system or vice versa; or they are intertwined in a complex relationship.

However, this assumed linkage between democracy and economic development is contradicted by the experiences of those East Asian countries under authoritarian rule. Unlike Japan, China is a one-party state with no election and its economic development is associated with authoritarian rule. Thus, for example, the former prime minister of Malaysia Dr Mahathir Mohamad has interpreted it to mean that a nation can develop well even in the absence of freedom, liberty and equality.[20] This in itself is not controversial in the sense that China is not an exceptional case. Authoritarian rule in some other East Asian countries has indeed produced impressive economic growth, even growth that has continued for a few decades. The bigger question is whether economic development is all that people yearn for. The question is all the more pertinent when the growth is based on continuously squeezing the poor, when it is accompanied

---

[19]Interestingly he feels that there is a stage-by-stage process in societal development. First, economic development, second individual freedom, third social justice and fourth political democracy. Source: 李泽厚，"政治民主不是非得马上实现"，南方人物周刊第20期，2010 年06月11日. (Li Zehou, "Political Democracy Needs Not be Realized Immediately", *Southern People Weekly*, No. 20, 11 June 2010, http://news.sina.com.cn/c/sd/2010-06-11/162620459655_4.shtml [accessed 2 December 2010].)

[20] "Mahathir Promotes China Model as Alternative to Democracy", *Today* (Singaporean newspaper), 19 October 2010.

by pollution of the environment, and when the state fails to channel resources to provide adequate basic social amenities like good education and healthcare.

A plausible conclusion is that economic development, at least to some extent, can be decoupled from the political system, at least for a considerable period. With special reference to China, there is this trenchant observation: "Post-Tiananmen Chinese governance is a model of market development administered by an autocratic state. It demythologizes the faith that capitalism is a socioeconomic force conducive to the flourish of democratic institutions, free and egalitarian societies. The short history of neoliberal capitalism since Tiananmen and the end of the Cold War has clearly disavowed the coupling between democracy and capitalism, and questions if the latter is the precondition of the former."[21]

This is not to claim that it is totally decoupled all the time. For example, in South Korea and Taiwan, democratic change seems to have happened after economic development has reached a certain stage. Another point is that economic development cannot keep on progressing without social development, for the latter will raise the level of human capital, skill level and quality of the workforce. At the same time, long-term authoritarian rule coupled with favouring the rich and powerful is bound to lead to social instability. In other words, in the long run social progress and evolution of the political system cannot be divorced from economic development.

There are market failures. There are issues of social welfare and national security that cannot be solved by markets, where the case for industrial policy is very clear. What is also very crucial is that markets can only operate properly under well-regulated institutions. However, there are areas where governments should stay away from. For example, the optimum size of a business and the merger decision of a firm are matters best left to the entrepreneurs concerned.[22]

One interesting insight gained from studying East Asian economic development is that state intervention and a market economy can co-exist and may indeed form a symbiotic relationship. One may even argue that this

---

[21]David Leiwei Li, "Remembrance Against Manufactured Amnesia: On the 20th Anniversary of the Tiananmen Incident", *Jump Cut — A Review of Contemporary Media*, 2009, http://www.ejumpcut.org/archive/jc51.2009/Tiananmen/index.html.
[22]杨沐, 产业政策研究 (上海: 三联出版社, 1989). (Yang Mu, *A Theoretical Study of Industrial Policy* (Shanghai: Sanlian Publishing House, 1989).)

does not contradict Adam Smith. Somehow Smith's discourse on the merits of the market has led to the interpretation that he rejects state intervention. This is an unfortunate misconception. He rejects only state interventions that exclude the market, not interventions that include the market while aiming to do those important things that the market may leave undone.[23]

Markets should not be seen to be in an antagonistic relationship with other social institutions operating in an open and free economy. Business firms, industrial associations and trade unions are all elements of such an economy and should be seen to be essential in promoting the operations of each other, rather than curbing the activities of each other. Richard Freeman makes this point very well in his "Conversations with History" programme hosted by the University of California at Berkeley, available on YouTube.[24]

Don't Forget the Context

It is almost trite to point out that economic development takes place within a concrete societal context with its culture, social makeup, existing infrastructure, history and international conditions. These are points that do not feature centrally in economic models for the simple reason that the concrete conditions are bound to change with time while models are supposed to be abstractions of useful experiences. Bearing this point in mind, it is useful to consider the economic conditions of China before the 1978 reform, the cultural background, social institutions and history, and international conditions.

This line of thinking is very much in the intellectual tradition followed by Fernand Braudel in his study of the rise of capitalism in Europe.[25] Going beyond Max Weber who focused on the role of cultural ideas in his famous study *The Protestant Ethic and the Spirit of Capitalism*, Braudel pays due

---

[23] Amartya Sen, "Capitalism Beyond the Crisis", *New York Review of Books*, 26 March 2009.

[24] "Global Capitalism, Labor Markets, and Inequality — Conversations host Harry Kreisler welcomes Harvard labor economist Richard B Freeman", 6 November 2007, http://www.google.com.sg/search?q=youtube+conversations+with+history+%2B+richard+freeman&hl=en&sa=G&prmd=ivnso&source=univ&tbs=vid:1&tbo=u&ei=Gv8aTdmDHIPKr-AfxuJ3bCw&oi=video_result_group&ct=title&resnum=1&ved=0CBcQqwQwAA [accessed 29 December 2010].

[25] Fernand Braudel, *Civilization and Capitalism 15th–18th Century*, Volumes 1–3 (New York: Harper & Row, 1979).

attention to the social networks forged among the emerging bourgeoisie during the religious wars. The social networks functioned as a kind of social infrastructure which promoted the commercial and subsequent industrial activities of the Protestant bourgeoisie.

Industrial Infrastructure Before the 1978 Reform

After the birth of the People's Republic of China, the leadership of the CPC formulated and implemented a set of policies to modernize the economy. Its leadership was fully aware that without a solid industrial base, it could not attain modernization. Looking back, we know that as far back as the 1960s, China's economic infrastructure was quite complex already and this laid the foundation for the country's future high growth.[26] However, subsequent modernization of the economy had to wait because of a combination of factors — the chaos of the Cultural Revolution, the boycott of the Soviet Union and the isolation in the context of the Cold War. Thus, it may be said that

"... while reforms after 1979 were important because they opened the economy and provided incentives for the private sector to develop, they could not have succeeded without acknowledging the stock of capabilities that existed in the country. ... Reforms toward a market system since the 1980s have been a key in China's development. However, we stress the path-dependent nature of development and emphasize the significant knowledge that had been accumulated before reforms started."[27]

This point is echoed by Wang Hui in his recent study of ongoing Chinese modernization.[28]

Quality of Workforce

It has been observed by many studies that transnational companies are attracted to invest in China because of its cheap labour and potential market of consumers. What is neglected is the quality of the labour force. The answer to this question is provided by Giovanni Arrighi. When he examines China's appeal to foreign transnational companies, he finds that "Contrary to widespread belief, the main attraction of the PRC for

---

[26] Jesus Felipe, Utsav Kumar, Norio Usui and Arnelyn Abdon, "Why Has China Succeeded — And Why It Will Continue to Do So", Levy Economics Institute Working Paper No. 611, 2010, p. 1.
[27] Ibid.
[28] Wang Hui, *The End of the Revolution* (London: Verso, 2009).

foreign capital has not been its huge and low-priced reserves of labor as such...The main attraction, we shall argue, has been the high quality of those reserves — in terms of health, education, and capacity for self-management — in combination with the rapid expansion of the supply and demand conditions."[29] Due attention to such important details is needed if we are to avoid the twin flaws of being too negative or too positive about others' experiences and one's own achievements.

Social Institutions and Networking

Every society exhibits some form of social networking, which is seen as a kind of social capital or cultural resource. Non-Chinese scholars and commentators often use the term *"guanxi"* or "relationships" to describe what appear to them as dense and mysterious social relationships in business activities in China. In reflecting on the record of economic development, Huang Ping points out something very similar to *guanxi*. He says, "Our strength lies in variegated ensembles of social organization. They include traditional organizations like families, relatives and clans, modern organizations like village committees, women associations and party branches, or new organizations like technical associations, farmer groups with special interests in seeds or pig rearing. Underpinning these bodies is a set of shared values and identity."[30]

One special kind of this social relationship is the network of overseas Chinese. Many of the older ones were born in China or have parents who were born in China and migrated abroad. It is natural for them to have some interests in China. So when China began its economic reform, the more entrepreneurial among them went to China to try their luck, and in the process contributed tremendously in the early phase. Though their roles have declined relative to those of transnational companies after China's accession to the WTO, they continue to actively participate in Chinese economic development.

The Chinese Consensus

Given the lukewarm reception among the Chinese of the Beijing Consensus, one wonders if there is some kind of consensus which holds the Chinese

---

[29] Giovanni Arrighi, *Adam Smith in Beijing* (London: Verso Books, 2008), p. 351.
[30] Huang Ping, "'Beijing Consensus' or 'Chinese Experience'?", Foreword to Huang Ping and Cui Zhi Wen (2005), p. 27.

together in their quest for industrialization, modernization and rapid economic growth. If there is, then the elements of the consensus need to have cultural and historical roots as well as a social basis. It may be argued that the ideas of national integrity and of *fuqiang* (meaning "wealth and power") fit this bill well.

A cursory reading of Chinese history reveals a clear pattern. A period of political stability soon after the birth of a new dynasty lasting for two to three centuries was followed by a period of national disintegration, chaos and disaster. The decline period could last for decades and brought immense suffering to the people, marked by a sharp drop in the population. With a long memory of their history transmitted through formal teaching, stories and dramas, the Chinese people have a deep-seated fear of chaos and disunity. In their assessment of political leaders, Chinese historians often use the criterion of a leader's ability to keep the whole country united, especially re-unity after a period of chaos and disintegration. Apart from chaos and human misery as a result of political fragmentation, there is the economic logic of water management.[31] The tasks of flood control of the river systems and ensuring equitable use of the water are much more manageable when the whole land mass is administered as a single political unit. One may thus say that there is a powerful rationale behind the Chinese desire or even national ideal of national integrity which dates back to at least the time of the Spring and Autumn Period (770–475 BCE).

The concept of *fuqiang* has a background of being a product of a violent period in Chinese history and was used to further imperialist tendencies by Japan.[32] But it carries a different connotation for contemporary China, with its century-long memory of humiliation suffered at the hand of foreign powers since the Opium War (1840–1842). The Opium War marked the beginning of a series of military aggressions by foreign powers against which China proved too weak to fight back. The upshot was that China was

---

[31] See, for example, Ray Huang, *China: A Macro History* (Armonk, NY: M.E. Sharpe, 1997); and Wang Gungwu, *Preparing for Reunification 883–947* (Singapore: World Scientific, 2007).

[32] The term *"fuqiang"* comes from the ancient phrase *"fuguo qiangbing"* — enriching the state and strengthening the armies. It was first used in the classic text *Chronicles of the Warring States* to describe the ideas of Shang Yang and his disciples. *Fuqiang* was extolled in the Meiji Revolution in Japan in the 19th century. *Fukoku kyohei* — Japanese for *fuguo qiangbing* — became Japan's national slogan in following the model of Western imperialism. The goals of government were modernized to seek wealth through industrialization and power through modern armaments. *Source*: Wang Gungwu, "China Needs to Stay True to Its Civilisation", *The Straits Times* 8 December 2010.

forced to sign unequal treaties, ceding extra-territorial rights to the victor countries and rights to build railways, to navigate freely in Chinese waters and to trade. In 1858, a contingent of British and French troops marched into Beijing and burned the imperial palace, inflicting deep wounds on the Chinese political psyche. Taiwan was seized by Japan in 1895, which turned the island into a full-fledged colony. Japan followed this up with outright invasion and occupation of northern and eastern China, and there was the brutal Massacre of Nanjing in 1937. School textbooks make it a point to remind the students of how the country had suffered at the hands of foreigners. Stories continue to be written and films made with such humiliating history as the background. There is thus a deeply felt desire among the Chinese people and government for the country to be strong, in order not to let such history repeat itself.

The twin concepts of *fuqiang* and national integrity may be the most unquestioned ideals of mainland Chinese across a broad political spectrum. These are ideals shared by both the CPC and KMT, providing a common language for Mao Zedong and Chiang Kai-shek. We can even call it the Chinese Consensus. As long as the CPC does well in these two aspects, the party can claim to have the political legitimacy to rule. This Consensus may help us understand the behaviour of the Beijing government, and the Chinese people's response to it. There is a danger, though, that the Chinese government may exploit the fear of the Chinese of chaos and instability, to tighten the screws whenever there are legitimate protests against abuse of powers, corruption, bureaucratic incompetence and squandering of public funds.

From the psychological aspect, the urge to get on better in life materially was suppressed for three long decades by the CPC. The economic reform promulgated in 1978 prompted a release of the pent-up desire to improve one's standard of living, which is a very normal human feeling. Combined with the slogan of "Getting rich first", the result has been nothing short of a feverish national movement to prove one's worth with material wealth. This has translated into impressive GDP figures and changes in the physical landscape — skyscrapers, high-speed rail, airports, factories and shopping malls. At the same time, we are witnessing some ugly social behaviour reminiscent of the behaviour of the *nouveau riche* often seen among the early bourgeoisie.

Learning from the Scandinavian Experience

As a complex phenomenon, capitalism has a few variants. We have the Japanese variant with a strong dose of state intervention, with other

East Asian countries exhibiting minor deviations from this variant. There is the Anglo-American variant which places faith in the wisdom of the market mechanism and allows lots of room for financial capital.

And there is the Scandinavian variant with its singular success in balancing social justice with market dynamism, flexibility with security, and economic growth with environmental protection. In the vast pool of Chinese economic literature documenting the experiences of other countries, the Nordic variant has received relatively less exposure. It may be argued that this variant has a lot to speak to the Chinese political and business leaders, workers and retired people. Following the fashion in describing developmental models, this variant has been called the Copenhagen Consensus, which happens to be the title of a neatly written article published in *Foreign Affairs*.[33] Though the research is based on empirical investigations in Denmark, the study reveals the essential features of other Scandinavian countries as well.

What is so remarkable about the Copenhagen Consensus? At first sight, it seems to be an impossible marriage of two conflicting socio-economic tendencies. Indeed it is a very original and skilful synthesis of what is economically desirable and socially desirable, exhibiting the high degree of wisdom of the people and their business and political leaders. Part of the article is as follows:

> On the one hand, the Danes are passionate free traders. They score well in the ratings constructed by pro-market organizations. The World Economic Forum's Global Competitiveness Index ranks Denmark third, just behind the United States and Switzerland. Denmark's financial markets are clean and transparent, its barriers to imports minimal, its labor markets the most flexible in Europe, its multinational corporations dynamic and largely unmolested by industrial policies, and its unemployment rate of 2.8 percent the second lowest in the OECD (the Organization for Economic Cooperation and Development).
>
> On the other hand, Denmark spends about 50 percent of its GDP on public outlays and has the world's second-highest tax rate, after Sweden; strong trade unions; and one of the world's most equal income distributions. For the half of GDP that they pay in taxes, the Danes get not just universal health insurance but also generous child-care and family-leave arrangements, unemployment compensation that typically covers around 95 percent of lost wages, free higher education, secure pensions in old age, and the world's most creative system of worker retraining.[34]

---

[33]Robert Kuttner, "The Copenhagen Consensus: Reading Adam Smith in Denmark", *Foreign Affairs*, Vol. 87, No. 2 (2008), p. 78.
[34]Ibid.

There are four additional indicators of the merits of the model. First, the productive workforce has produced world-class firms like Oticon, Bang & Olufsen, Novo Nordisk and Maersk. Second, the country has a good record of environmental protection. Third, it has low crime rates. Fourth, it contributes generously to the poorer countries.

The Danish model is part of the social system which began with the win-win compromise between labour and capital in 1899. In other words, it is the product of a century-long evolution of its politics and culture. It is a manifestation of a broad national commitment to two socio-economic goals, namely, (1) a highly egalitarian society, and (2) the use of ongoing labour-market subsidies to create a highly skilled and dynamic workforce as the essence of global competitiveness. It is a concrete example of the ideals propounded by Plato and Aristotle that economy is part of society and economic development must serve social development.[35] It is a characteristic of what may be called rich societal resources, which we have treated elsewhere.[36] Societal resources are more than what is called social capital.[37] They refer to the cultural and moral tolerance and vitality of a society, intellectual openness and ferment,[38] and social cohesion and harmony. They provide the basis for social justice and economic dynamism. They not only take the form of individual beliefs and behaviours but are also embedded in social institutions. Examples of poverty in societal resources are gun-related violence and drug abuse, rampant corruption, grave income disparity and child abuse. Denmark exhibits many of the positive attributes of rich societal resources, although it is currently being confronted with the problems associated with an influx of immigrants.[39]

Programme of Non-stop Learning

It has been observed elsewhere in this book that a key feature of China's economic development is the country's openness and willingness to learn

---

[35]Hsieh Ching-Yao and Ye Meng-Hua, *Economics, Philosophy, and Physics* (Armonk, NY: M.E. Sharpe, 1991).

[36]Michael Heng Siam-Heng, *The Great Recession: History, Ideology, Hubris and Nemesis* (Singapore: World Scientific, 2010).

[37]See, for example, Robert Putnam, *Bowling Alone: The Collapse and Revival of American Community* (New York: Simon and Schuster, 2000).

[38]Manifestations of such intellectual vigour are often seen in literature, fine arts, science and philosophy.

[39]Robert Kuttner, "The Copenhagen Consensus: Reading Adam Smith in Denmark", *Foreign Affairs*, Vol. 87, No. 2 (2008), p. 78.

from others. If that history is a reliable guide, it is safe to assume that China will continue to learn from others in the future. The need to do so is obviously there. In terms of GDP per capita, China is still far behind others, ranking 95th in the list prepared by the IMF.[40]

In the wake of the 2008 financial crisis, there has been intense interest in the robust recovery and even remarkable economic performance of not only China, but also South Korea and India. Such interest has inspired the concepts of the Seoul Consensus and the Mumbai Consensus. The former refers to strong, sustainable, inclusive and resilient growth,[41] while the latter refers to the idea of a democratic developmental state, driven by a people-centred emphasis on growing levels of consumption and a widening middle class.[42]

Beyond the catchy name of the Seoul Consensus, South Korea has demonstrated some capacities that Beijing may like to study. Its economy was brought low by the 1997 Asian financial crisis. But it bounced back quickly. What amazed the world was the solidarity of the ordinary people, as shown by women donating their jewellery, and engineers working long hours and even living in the factories to rebuild the economy. It was a case of national solidarity transformed into economic resolve and strength. Today South Korea can rightly boast of several technology-based companies of world-class stature, like Samsung, LG and Hyundai. Its once tarnished *chaebol* are now standing tall, a case study for developing countries to learn how to nurture competitive transnational companies.

On its part, India has made a name for itself in growing its IT industry, both in terms of software and IT services. A truly pluralistic society, it is also a continental-sized country with a population approaching that of China. Its economic growth is thus at the same time a growth in its ability to cope with the immense complexities originating in its sheer size and

---

[40]List of countries by GDP (nominal) per capita, http://en.wikipedia.org/wiki/List_of_countries_by_GDP_(nominal)_per_capita [accessed 15 January 2011].

[41]"A More Optimistic Take on the 'Seoul Consensus'", International Political Economy Zone, 17 November 2010, http://ipezone.blogspot.com/2010/11/more-optimistic-take-on-seoul-consensus.html [accessed 30 November 2010]. "Meet the 'Seoul Consensus'", International Political Economy Zone, 12 November 2010, http://ipezone.blogspot.com/2010/11/meet-seoul-consensus-enough-dc-beijing.html [accessed 30 November 2010].

[42]Lawrence H. Summers, "India and the Global Economy", 15 October 2010, http://www.whitehouse.gov/administration/eop/nec/speeches/india-global-economy [accessed 14 January 2011]. Chrystia Freeland, "The Mumbai Consensus", Reuters, 22 October 2010, http://blogs.reuters.com/chrystia-freeland/2010/10/22/the-mumbai-consensus/ [accessed 14 January 2011].

dazzling pluralism. Its modernization experience is also a splendid record of reconciling the local with the foreign, the traditional with the modern, and what is more, how these "opposing" elements are transformed in the process of meeting, collision, conversation, negotiation and synthesis.

Just like India, China encounters special issues arising from its size and long history, with their pluses and minuses. They are of a higher order of complexity not faced by small and medium-sized countries. In this sense, China's successes and failures must be examined with this point in mind. In other words, insights based on the Chinese experience may not always be relevant for other countries with a much smaller geographical spread and population, and smaller historical burdens. This is one crucial dimension that discussions on the Washington Consensus and the Beijing Consensus have somehow neglected.

Every country has to find its own set of answers to the problem of how to grow its economy while taking care of social stability, physical environment, political progress and national security. It is certainly not a simple endeavour. Attractive and powerful lessons from elsewhere, when applied, may encounter historical burdens and constraints imposed by the social and political realities. As pointed out earlier in this chapter, it is a process of institutional learning, of trial and error, of cautious experimentation and of social engineering. In a very real sense, it is a leap into the unknown. Success depends not only on cultural and intellectual resources, political leadership and wisdom, social solidarity, and geographical and historical advantages, but also on international conditions and good luck. Viewed in this light, there is no royal road to economic development, and a neatly formulated model in the form of a consensus is a roadmap which may turn out to be a shortcut to the wrong destination.

Chapter Eight

By Way of Conclusion:
Some Random Thoughts

Introduction: Challenges Ahead

In the closing chapter of this book, perhaps we can indulge in forward-looking, tentative, random thoughts. We would like to discuss the way forward for the Chinese economy. But to do so, we need to lay down the parameters which guide our thinking.

It is obvious that there has been remarkable economic development in China, lifting hundreds of millions out of abject poverty. A large body of literature documents the achievements since the reform in 1978. With China coping fairly well with the 2008 financial crisis, in contrast to the continuing woes of the West, the tone of the writings has become even more laudatory.[1] However, in the good Chinese tradition of keeping one's head cool in the face of success, it is useful to take note of some important facts.

First, how much of the GDP growth is due to real growth? In terms of real purchasing power, 10,000 yuan in 2010 is worth only as much as 125 yuan was worth 30 years ago. If this is factored in, the real annual GDP growth of China is certainly smaller than the double-digit growth figures that appear so often in news reports, commentaries and books. In addition, some of the growth is accounted for by wasteful investment. The most blatant example is putting up a building, only to tear it down not long afterwards. Judging from reports available on the Internet, the practice is quite widespread, even though there has been no systematic study done to produce concrete figures.

Second, a more serious issue is structural in nature, namely the composition of the population. China has been benefiting from what is known as demographic dividends, namely a high percentage of people of working age relative to the percentage of dependants. In years to come, these benefits will morph into the opposite — an increasing number of

---

[1] Martin Jacques, *When China Rules the World* (London: Penguin, 2009).

old retired people supported by a shrinking workforce.[2] This is a problem currently faced by Japan and some European countries.

Third, the past continuous and steady economic growth for 32 years is in itself no guarantee that the next few decades will witness a similar performance. China needs to look no further than at its neighbour to know that the future can hold some nasty surprises. By most criteria, Japan had a record-breaking growth from the early 1950s to 1990, just before its superbubble burst. The event ushered in a recession that still continues today.[3]

Fourth, the current model is not sustainable. It is mainly based on cheap labour and scant attention to the environment in agriculture, manufacturing and extraction of natural resources. Waterways are polluted. So is the air, especially in urban areas. The major cities are among the most polluted in the world. There are clear signs of rising labour costs in the eastern coastal regions. Exploitation of natural resources has not only led to depletion of the resources but also adverse impacts on the environment. A case in point is the mining and refinery of rare earth elements for export. Refining rare earth ore has very adverse impacts on the environment as it usually leaves thousands of tons of low-level radioactive waste behind. For good GDP figures, China has been prepared to do the dirty work. Processing factories in China "are barely regulated and in some cases illegally operated, and have created vast toxic waste sites".[4]

Given these problems, serious students of the Chinese economy are aware that the country must reformulate its economic strategy if it is to continue its robust economic growth. According to an influential economist in Beijing, "China's progress over the past three decades is

---

[2]Sharon LaFraniere, "As China Ages, Birthrate Policy May Prove Difficult to Reverse", *The New York Times*, 6 April 2011.

[3]With some modifications, similar comments could be made about the long boom in Indonesia until the Asian financial crisis in 1997, the long boom in the USA until the Great Depression in the 1930s, and the long boom in Mexico until the financial crisis in 1982.

[4]"Breaking China's Grip on Supplies of Rare Earths", *International Herald Tribune*, 8 March 2011, http://sarbjit.posterous.com/breaking-chinas-grip-on-supplies-of-rare-eart. According to the same report, China imposed in September 2010 a two-month embargo on rare earth shipments to Japan during a territorial dispute, and for a short time even blocked some shipments to the United States and Europe. The action has helped propel world prices of the material to record highs. Even with such high prices, countries with their rare earth ore deposits are not always eager to play host to the refineries that process them.

a successful variation on the East Asian growth model that stems from the initial conditions bequeathed by a planned socialist economy. That growth model has now almost exhausted its potential. So China has reached a crucial juncture: without painful structural adjustment, its economic-growth momentum can suddenly be lost."[5]

Closely related to economic development are the social and political issues. Two important issues are rampant corruption and income disparity. Corruption has reached all levels of government and the ruling Communist Party of China. According to the Chinese Academy of Social Sciences, around 800 billion yuan has been transferred overseas by officials and company executives who have fled the country since the mid-1990s.[6] Much more is believed to have been likely squirrelled away or spent on banquets, second homes and lovers inside China.[7] A recent case involved the railway minister, Liu Zhijun, who was accused of receiving 1 billion yuan. Numerous calls and stern warnings have been issued by the CPC and government; campaigns have been launched, and high officials convicted of serious corruption are jailed or even executed. All these have yielded few real tangible results. The problem is persistent with no end of it in sight.

The income disparity is growing. This problem becomes extra serious when the state, claiming to be ideologically guided by socialist ideals, has not done enough to redress healthcare, education and housing problems of the poor. The Gini coefficient has increased from 0.2 in the pre-reform period to 0.45 in early 2000; it has reached a point considered dangerous by the World Bank.[8]

Given the achievements of China so far, together with its teething problems, what is the way forward? We propose using the following rather non-controversial concepts as the starting point: (1) value-adding economic activities form a solid basis of economic growth and this must be given due attention in the context of fierce global competition, (2) long-term economic development can only happen in a physically healthy, psychologically

---

[5] Yu Yongding, "China Going Forward", Project Syndicate, 13 December 2010, http://www.project-syndicate.org/commentary/yu4/English [accessed 20 December 2010].
[6] Kenneth Rapoza, "Where Corrupt Chinese Hide Their Cash ... and Themselves", *Forbes*, 15 June 2011, http://blogs.forbes.com/kenrapoza/2011/06/15/where-corrupt-chinese-hide-their-cash-and-themselves/ [accessed 2 July 2011].
[7] "Chinese President Hu Jintao's Warning as Communist Party Celebrates 90 Years", *Guardian*, 1 July 2011, http://www.guardian.co.uk/world/2011/jul/01/chinese-president-corruption-communist-party [accessed 2 July 2011].
[8] 唐晋 (主编), 大国策: 经济模式 (北京: 人民出版社, 2009). (Tang Jin (ed.), *Big Power Strategy: Economic Models* (Beijing: Renmin Publishing House, 2009), p. 47.)

pleasant and socially peaceful environment, and (3) China has its own specific conditions, e.g. population size, geographical spread and diversity.

As the new decade begins, there are clear signs of strain and pressure within the Chinese economy. These signs are not much noticed among those who have profited greatly from the growth and those who feel proud of China's economic achievements. Given the circumstances they are in, they can be self-congratulatory. However, the more thoughtful Chinese are not so confident or complacent. They are fully aware of the backwardness of most parts of China, and that in terms of per capita GDP at purchasing power parity, China is ranked 94th, far below many other countries.[9]

Fundamentals of Long-Term Economic Growth

At this stage of China's economic development, growth is necessary to further uplift the living conditions of vast majority of the people. And this growth is best predicated on an increase in productivity, technological and social innovations, improving environmental conditions, and efficient consumption of energy and other raw materials. These are economic fundamentals for sustainable economic development.

GDP is the standard indicator used to express economic development. Social scientists rely on GDP figures to compare the economic achievements of different economies. Political analysts use GDP figures to compare the economic performance of different countries. In doing so, they may miss some salient points. For one thing, GDP can register a positive gain without any real economic development on the ground. For example, tearing down a new building and subsequently building a similar one contributes to GDP growth, but nothing to the real economy. We may even argue that its contribution is negative by virtue of its adverse impact on the physical environment.

Instead of GDP, it is more rewarding to think in terms of *value-creating* economic activities. To explain this concept, we have to go to the fundamentals of economic life. The concept is difficult to define, but we hope to provide a fair understanding of it by way of illustration. Suppose person A is using her mathematical talents in a research study to understand the life history of an infectious disease. Another equally intelligent person, B, is using his talents in a Wall Street firm to devise fancy derivative products

---

[9]List of countries by GDP (PPP) per capita, http://en.wikipedia.org/wiki/List_of_countries_by_GDP_(PPP)_per_capita [accessed 17 May 2011].

based on subprime mortgages. We may say person A is engaging in value-creating activity while person B is engaging in value-destroying activity. The recent financial crisis has highlighted the damage caused by financial speculation. To build a robust modern economy, China can learn much from the long experience of the free market economy of the West, so as to prevent financial speculation from running wild. The principal merit of a financial market is efficient allocation of financial resources, which entails some risk. But this risk is different in nature to that associated with financial speculation.

From the perspective of a market economy, the criterion of value-creating by a business project is not the only condition for embarking on the project. The project must also fulfil an additional critical condition, namely, there must be a pool of willing buyers who are able to pay for the goods or services.

A concept closely related to value creation is *productivity*, which has received a lot of attention in economics literature. However, increased productivity is not the same as value-adding. For example, productivity increase in manufacturing weapons in one country which uses it to commit acts of aggression is certainly not value-adding.

Productivity is the result of technological innovation or improved techniques to manage human resources, land and capital. In layman language, productivity measures how much output (product or service) is generated per unit of input (of resources, be it labour or capital). Productivity is seen as the key factor in explaining the long-term economic growth of a country. Its importance can be seen in the following passage in a well-known textbook: "Over long periods of time, small differences in rates of productivity growth compound, like interest in a bank account, and can make an enormous difference to a society's prosperity. Nothing contributes more to reduction of poverty, to increases in leisure, and to the country's ability to finance education, public health, environment and the arts."[10] This statement is certainly true. However, in the context of globalization, we need to consider another factor: *cost of production*. Take the case of America, whose productivity recorded an increase of 83 percent from 1973 to 2007 while the median real wage of men increased only by 5 percent.[11] The productivity increase was partly a response to competition from

---

[10] Alan Blinder and William Baumol, *Economics: Principles and Policy* (San Diego: Harcourt Brace Jovanovich, 1993), p. 778.
[11] "Marx, Mervyn or Mario?", *The Economist*, 24 March 2011.

abroad, but the increase was not big enough to bring about a corresponding increase in profitability. Neither could the US productivity increase arrest the decline in competitiveness of its manufacturing.[12] Competitiveness certainly depends on productivity, but to business enterprises, cost of production is an even more important measure. Consider the case of an American worker who is paid ten times the salary earned by his Chinese counterpart for the same work. The American worker may well be five times as productive but transnational companies will prefer to hire the Chinese worker, all other factors being equal.

What does this discussion hold for the Chinese economy? In the short term, China has much to offer in terms of cheap land and cheap skilled and unskilled labour. But with three decades of rapid economic growth, the supply of cheap labour is drying up. This shortage has manifested in the form of higher wages in the coastal areas.

In the medium and longer terms, China has to rely on innovation to increase its productivity, guided by the principle of adding value to society. So the passage quoted earlier about the crucial importance of productivity is certainly valid. By innovation, we follow Joseph Schumpeter who uses the term to refer to both technological and social innovation.[13] Schumpeter describes innovation as follows: (1) the introduction of new goods, (2) the introduction of new production methods, which may be based on scientific discovery, (3) the development of new sources of new materials, (4) the development of new markets, and (5) the creation of new organizational forms.

The first three kinds of innovation may be seen to fall under technological innovation. The widespread acceptance of technological innovation is a testimony to the intellectual contribution of Schumpeter and his like-minded economists. There is a huge body of literature on technological innovation, and it has become common knowledge that technology forms one of the pillars of economic prowess.[14] This idea was explicitly incorporated into the 12th Five-Year Plan for the economic development of China.

---

[12]Martijn Konings, "The United States in the Post-War Global Political Economy: Another Look at the Brenner Debate", in David Coates (ed.), *Varieties of Capitalism, Varieties of Approach* (New York: Palgrave, 2005).

Michael Heng Siam-Heng, *The Great Recession: History, Ideology, Hubris and Nemesis* (Singapore: World Scientific, 2010).

[13]Joseph Schumpeter, *The Theory of Economic Development* (Boston: Harvard University Press, 1934).

[14]See, for example, Adam Segal, *Advantage: How American Innovation Can Overcome the Asian Challenge* (New York: W. W. Norton, 2011).

The Roles of Social Innovation

In comparison to technological innovation, there is less interest in innovation in social organization, and this is reflected in the literature and academic and public discussions. Broadly defined, social organization refers to the way people are organized to achieve certain goals. Social innovations draw on the social, moral, cultural and historical resources of the society, and involve a process of experimentation and learning. Breakthroughs in social organization are placed by Kennedy in the same category as breakthroughs in technology in his study of the rise of powerful states.[15]

Here are some examples of social innovation. At the societal level, one important innovation is the development of the market as a socio-economic institution. At the organizational level, students and teachers know quite well from their experience that beyond a certain class size, teaching and learning can be difficult. In the business world, Ford and General Motors in the past and Google and Apple now are known for their social innovation. Business management literature has devoted keen attention to this aspect of Japanese companies, either in the form of collective responsibility on the shop floor or business networks like *keiretsu*.[16]

Compared to other nations, China is a relative newcomer to industrialization and modernization. Technological systems can be relatively easily transplanted from foreign sources, but it is much more difficult to do so with social organizations from foreign cultural soils. While being open to foreign sources, Chinese social entrepreneurs can think of nurturing and promoting the organic growth of indigenous social organizations in their own cultural milieu. In this period of profound economic transformation, there is much scope for social innovation at the organizational level and societal level. Social innovation releases creative energies as much as technological innovation releases nature's capabilities. Business leaders and political leaders have to be persuaded in this so that they can be actively engaged in supporting it.

---

[15]Paul Kennedy, *The Rise and Fall of the Great Powers* (London: Fontana, 1989).

[16]A *keiretsu* is an example of social innovation at the industrial level. It is a social organization in the business world which is based on the bedrock of cultural resources and value systems. Another example is an industrial association which functions as a representative body for their members in the same industry and as an information hub. If it functions as a self-governing body with the power to impose discipline, it can enhance the professional standing of the profession, e.g. a professional association of medical doctors.

Here we would like to give a simple example of how a government can undertake a project of social innovation at the societal level. Business organizations, being what they are, are not so concerned with issues beyond the boundaries of their organizations.[17] They are not too concerned about their employees having to spend hours commuting to work. In cities, it is common for people to spend two hours going to work and two hours going home. Spending four hours on the road is a great waste of time. It deprives those with families of quality time with their family members. Moreover, it is frustrating psychologically and exhausting physically. It increases the level of air pollution and cost of living. It is here that town and city governments have to step in to provide the infrastructure for mass transport. These problems are acute in megacities.

Until recently, megacities formed part of a common trend of urbanization in the West. China is in the process of catching up. Rapid urbanization comes with many opportunities and problems. Towns and cities have historically grown from market centres or administration centres or meeting points of major transport routes. By attracting different people to the same physical location, they represent a pool of skills, a reservoir of creativity, social interaction and cultural diversity. They provide opportunities for cultural creation, scientific advancement and technological innovation. Businesses are attracted to such urban centres as sources of human skills and markets for their products. The result is a social dynamic conducive to creativity, resulting in wealth creation, cultural production and intellectual vibrancy. Cities have become the natural centres of economic and political powers. Powerful interest groups can provide the momentum for city expansion.

But cities do have downsides, and these are especially pronounced in megacities. The problem is particularly serious when they are situated in unsuitable geographical places. For example, Beijing with its 22 million people and Tianjin with its 12 million people have drained underground aquifers that took thousands of years to form.[18] In a biological sense,

---

[17]Business organizations are in the habit of getting their employees to work overtime, instead of recruiting more workforce to do the work, all in the name of flexibility. (In the worst-case scenario, they do not even pay for the overtime work.) This transfer of burden to employees has an obvious cost to the employees as private individuals. Moreover, it entails a hidden cost to society. For example, overstressed employees may give up the idea of having babies.

[18] "A Thirsty North Looks Southward in China", *International Herald Tribune*, 2 June 2011.

cities are not self-sustaining systems. They rely on rural areas as suppliers of food. At the same time, cities produce tremendous amounts of waste. Beyond a certain size (usually measured in terms of population), they will create problems that undermine the merits of city life and are counterproductive. Well-known problems are traffic congestion, pollution, waste, excessive energy consumption, pressure on the infrastructure and crime. The infrastructure cost per person also increases with increasing size. Moreover, given the dense population and tightly integrated transport systems, megacities tend to attract terrorist attacks.

Another study adds: "Megacities are also focuses of global risk. They are increasingly vulnerable systems because they often harbor pronounced poverty, social inequality and environmental degradation, all of which are linked together by a complex system supplying goods and services. People from different socio-economic groups and corresponding political allegiances may become segregated geographically, creating disparities and conflict. Population density increases vulnerability to natural and manmade hazards. Thus, megacities, exposed to the global environmental, socio-economic and political changes to which they contribute, are both victims and producers of risk."[19]

The critical perspective on megacities is very much in line with our understanding of the need to protect the environment.

This is a powerful guiding principle that has emerged in the course of rising awareness of the ecological degradation due to industrialization, mining, deforestation and intensive farming. The negative impacts of economic development on the physical environment have received lots of coverage in the press and research literature. We shall therefore not go through them again here.

Chinese megacities like Beijing and Shanghai exhibit many of these problems. Before they grow even more to become too big to manage, it would be fruitful to sit back and reconsider alternatives to urbanization, to leverage on the capabilities of new information technologies and transport systems like high-speed rail. Unlike many developing countries, China has a web of high-speed railways and highways; they should be used as a basic physical infrastructure to design town and cities — a design that moves away from the model of megacities. From the viewpoint of social equity,

---

[19]Frauke Kraas, "Megacities — Our Global Urban Future", EUcommerz, 4 September 2008, http://www.eucommerz.com/a/0063_megacities_our_global_urban_future [accessed 5 October 2010].

this will help to narrow the gap currently existing between the rural folks and urbanites.

In regions with high economic potential, a system of small and medium-sized towns and cities linked by high-speed Internet and rail offers a powerful alternative. In small towns, people can walk or cycle to work. This not only reduces traffic congestion and air pollution, but is also very important in coping with the spread of airborne diseases, especially during times of epidemics. One innovation along this line of thinking is the concept of rubanization.[20]

Efficient Use of Natural Resources

The issue of megacities discussed in the previous section illustrates also the importance of efficient use of natural resources. Cities should not be so big that they impose too heavy an ecological burden. The location of a city should be chosen with this in mind. The same thinking applies to the location and size of manufacturing facilities. However, political consideration often subverts such rationality. One such example is the construction of a multi-billion-dollar semiconductor plant in Beijing. The manufacture of semiconductors needs lots of water and the surrounding air must be relatively dust-free. Beijing does not meet these conditions. Besides adding to pressure on the environment, locating such plants in the Beijing area adds to the cost of production.

The issue of efficient use of natural resources has become more important as more developing countries are slowly catching up with the rich countries. There is an increasing demand for commodities. This translates into higher commodity prices on the world market as well as more pollution. Loud voices have been raised to ask China to reduce its greenhouse gas emissions and to tackle pollution. The simple fact is that the greenhouse gas emissions per capita in China is far below that in the USA. It is morally indefensible to ask an average Chinese to give up his quest for better living conditions while an average American is consuming a few dozen times more.

---

[20] In a nutshell, rubanization proposes building small townships with residential housing, schools, polyclinics, factories, offices, shopping facilities and cultural amenities. Residents in the township can walk or cycle to school or the workplace. The small towns are separated by vegetable farms, fruit gardens and trees which consume the organic waste produced, but are connected by roads and railways. See more on rubanization at http://www.rubanisation.org/.

Having made this point, it must be added that China should not try to emulate the wasteful habits of others. Rather, China can learn much from Japan in trying to be very efficient in its use of natural resources. Here, scientific advances and technological innovations offer a solution. Another is adopting a lifestyle that is more in tune with the times.

One aspect of modern life deserves special attention, and that is the use of cars, and related to it is the automobile industry. In an interesting way, the car industry can excite leaders of many developing countries, and here we shall dwell on two points.[21] The first is that the car industry is considered a symbol of industrial prowess and vitality. It is an image that emerged during the early part of the previous century. Though the Western world no longer sees it as an icon of industrial vitality, the old image dies hard amongst leaders of developing countries. For sure, car manufacturing is a big boy in many countries. Together with related industries supporting car manufacturing, one can think of millions of jobs associated with it. Moreover, the car industry provides an industrial base for the manufacture of armoured vehicles, and is therefore important for national defense. This much is obvious and non-controversial.

Second is the promotion of the use of cars, especially when it is done at the expense of alternative forms of transport like public transport and cycling. Most of us are aware of the evident costs of such a development: traffic congestion, land used for roads and parking lots, time wasted in commuting and air pollution. In the long run, what is even more dangerous is the addiction to petroleum. The USA has been on this path long enough for the world to see its adverse consequences. Even though the addiction has grave economic and geopolitical consequences, the USA is finding it very difficult to wean the people off it.[22] In the competition for resources, energy is of special importance. Looking further ahead, it does not make sense for China to promote widespread use of cars, for it can only deepen its dependence on oil imports, putting it in a more vulnerable position, especially in times of supply shortfall and in times of international tension.

In contrast to the promotion of cars is the use of high-speed rail. Given the huge population in China and the vast expanse of the country, a high-speed rail system has a lot to be commended for. It is safe, fast,

---

[21]For example, Malaysia has at great cost created its own car manufacturing industry.
[22]Thomas Friedman, *Hot, Flat and Crowded* (London: Allen Lane, 2008). Friedman repeats this point many times in his regular columns in the *International Herald Tribune*.

comfortable and reliable, and transports large numbers of passengers. It is more energy-efficient than car travel, and certainly much more than air travel.

Specific Conditions of China

The main reason economic development in China is so important for the world is its size — both in terms of its population and geography. A significant increase in its imports or exports will directly affect the rest of the world economy. Size carries with it special responsibility. One example is in food security. It has been argued that China must achieve more or less self-sufficiency in food production, both for its own good and for the rest of the world.[23] For China itself, size has a few advantages that small countries do not enjoy.

The first advantage is the scope it offers in learning. It can try out at the same time different strategies in industrial policies. Some provinces can try out an industrial policy that gives more emphasis to supporting the small and medium-sized enterprises. SMEs are socially and politically important because they make up 99 percent of the enterprises.[24] They are an important provider of employment; they are flexible and are very cost-conscious. They are usually privately owned, which means that they are not at the mercy of the vagaries of stock market sentiments. State support can take various forms. For example, the state can either set up state banks or allow private initiatives to set up banks to cater to the needs of small businesses and medium-sized businesses respectively. SMEs are not served by the major state-owned banks. Small businesses have to turn to each other for financial assistance, or to high-interest underground lenders.[25] The state can also help where the task is beyond the capacity of any individual SME, e.g. by funding research in universities that will benefit the whole industry, or assisting in the exploration of markets.

---

[23] John Wong, "Self-sufficient Food Policy Benefits World", *China Daily*, 31 May 2011, http://www.chinadaily.com.cn/bizchina/2011-05/31/content_12613499.htm [accessed 2 June 2011].

[24] A medium-sized enterprise employs up to 3,000 people while a small enterprise can employ ten or less persons. Source: 张维迎 (主编), 金融危机后的中国经济 (上海: 人民出版社, 2010), p. 22. (Zhang Weiying (ed.), *Chinese Economy after the Financial Crisis* (Shanghai: People's Publishing Press, 2010), p. 22.)

[25] Ibid., p. 23.

While some provinces focus on nurturing nimble and enterprising SMEs, some other provinces can adopt an industrial policy to nurture huge industrial concerns similar to that pursued by the Seoul government in assisting *chaebol*. Traditionally the Chinese government has been focusing on SOEs. It is true that SOEs provide employment and run businesses that are of vital national interest. But they suffer from the usual shortcomings found in monopolies or quasi-monopolies. They tend to wield undue political influence which allows them to distort rational economic decision making. There is the pitfall of inefficiency. As a country advances in its quest to become a more market-oriented economy, the role of the state should be to create a climate for the germination and healthy growth of private transnational companies.[26]

There is an area where supporting SMEs and nurturing transnational companies do not come into conflict. The state can assume the responsibility (especially the financial costs) of supplying useful market information to its business community or of providing the basic physical infrastructure. For example, it would do well to pay attention to market failures.[27] This is why diversification and discovery are more likely to happen in a market economy with *some kind* of government action.

The second advantage is the capacity to learn from the whole world. The state can afford to send students literally to universities in all foreign countries in order to learn firsthand the languages, cultures, business practices and systems. Unfortunately, Chinese students are too narrowly focused on the USA as a destination of learning. Here, the state and businesses can step in to correct such bias by way of providing scholarships and encouragement.

The third advantage is the potential of a huge market which enterprising businesses can use to develop technical standards. This advantage has been used by American technological companies, allowing them to set standards for the rest of the world to follow. At this point of writing, China still does not possess the technological prowess and market size to exploit this advantage.

The fourth advantage is that an economy of continental size can offer a higher degree of isolating protection against the ups and downs of the global market. This point can clearly be seen in the recent financial crisis.

---

[26] Jesus Felipe, Utsav Kumar, Norio Usui and Arnelyn Abdon, "Why Has China Succeeded — And Why It Will Continue to Do So", Levy Economics Institute Working Paper No. 611, 2010.
[27] Ibid.

Taxation, Corruption and All That

A number of economic issues have been making the news. They are rampant corruption, high cost of housing, debts taken on by local governments, inadequate social safety nets, and social unrest. We shall argue that these issues are closely related. One common factor needed in tackling them is strong financial resources of the central government. To clarify, we are not saying that it is the only factor. Other factors such as a capable and committed political leadership, political reform and institutional building are crucial too. But we will not dwell on these other factors as they are outside the scope of the book.

The next question is: how can the government raise the money? Luckily in China, there are avenues where the state can raise money through taxation. It has been argued that heavy and progressive tax should be imposed on luxury goods and services like yachts, private jets, membership of exclusive clubs, paintings, antiques and upmarket residences.[28] Other targets are speculative activities like buying and selling of real estate, and stocks bought and sold within a short period. As part of good governance, the central state government must explain the rationale behind the taxation.

Part of the money must be used to increase the pay of the civil servants. As it is quite well-known, the official pay of employees working in government bodies is too low. The honest ones are forced by their dire circumstances to take up a second job in order to make ends meet. For example, teachers give private tuition classes. Such economic conditions give rise to undesirable social practices, like doctors receiving *hongbao* (cash put in red envelopes) from patients. Worse still, it gives rise to pervasive bribery. This is especially so when senior leaders and their relatives are known to be on the take. This greatly weakens whatever deterrent effect that anti-corruption legislatures may have on other government officials and party cadres.[29] The upshot is a system-wide social disease that has almost become a habit. It has deeply eroded public respect for CPC members

---

[28]杨沐，"开征奢侈消费税，专项用于扶贫"，林双林，刘怡，钱立 (主编)，中国社会保障制度探索 (北京：中国财政经济出版社, 2008). (Yang Mu, "Impose Consumer Tax on Luxury Goods and Use It to Assist the Poor", in Lin Shuang Lin, Liu Yi and Qian Li (eds.), *An Exploratory Study of Chinese Social Security System* (Beijing: China Finance and Economics Publishing House, 2008).)

[29]The Chinese have a beautiful expression to describe this: 上梁不正，下梁歪 (If the leaders do not behave well, those below will do likewise).

and confidence in the government. The situation has become so serious that state and party leaders have repeatedly issued stern warnings that corruption can lead to the collapse of the CPC rule.

The problem of corruption is a perennial theme in Chinese history. History books and popular stories carry vivid accounts of how corruption amongst the ruling elite and mandarins was one of the key factors leading to the downfall of a previously powerful dynasty. Obviously, corruption happens not because they are Chinese, for Hong Kong and Singapore with their Chinese majorities have clean governments. India, Indonesia, Malaysia, the Philippines and many other non-Chinese countries are also well-known for corruption. The political system alone cannot explain the story. Some democracies are very corrupt and some are not. Poor salary is a condition for corruption, and this fact was demonstrated in the Ming Dynasty. Its founding emperor Zhu Yuanzhang was allergic to corruption and he meted out the most severe punishment to those convicted of the crime, but to no avail. The simple answer was that his mandarins were too poorly paid. The lesson to draw from this is that the Chinese officials should be better paid, not at the level of their counterparts in the business sector, but enough for them to live in modest material comfort and security. At the same time, they are required to live on that salary alone. For the top leaders during their term of office, their children are not allowed to run businesses.

A clean government has an immense impact on social stability, regime legitimacy and economic development. It has the potential to break the vicious cycle of corruption, abuse of power, waste and social unrest. As an indication of how the government perceives the threat of social unrest, the 2011 budget allocates more money to domestic security than to national defense.[30]

With reductions in waste, improved efficiency and less expenditure on curbing social unrest, the extra money can be channelled to the local governments. Inadequate funding for local governments increases the danger of the central government losing control of the local governments. It is also a key reason why local governments are actively involved in seizing land from peasants for housing construction: as a source of income. This

---

[30]The amount allocated for public security is 624 billion yuan; for defense, 601 billion yuan; for medical and healthcare, 536 billion yuan; for low-income housing, 103 billion yuan. "FACTBOX — Selected Figures from China's 2011 Budget", http://www.xe.com/news/2011-03-05%2000:36:00.0/1746569.htm [accessed 15 June 2011].

leads to collusion between developers and local governments in a game that manifests itself as social unrest and a housing bubble.[31] By any measure, there is a housing bubble in China.[32] Its bursting is not likely to give rise to a recession as in the USA and Japan, but it is bound to cause unnecessary hardship to honest owners who buy at the peak and to banks in the housing loan business. Labour and material costs account for only a small fraction of the current price of apartments in the major cities. The difference between the construction cost and house price is accounted for by the land cost (which goes to the local government) and developers' profits. Solving the housing problem will reduce another major source of social discontent. It will also correct a distortion in investment by state-owned companies. Chinese state-owned banks gave out huge loans to state-owned enterprises as part of the stimulus strategy to reduce the impact of the global financial crisis. But many of these loans ended up going to real estate purchases instead.[33]

Another issue fuelling social discontent is in the areas of healthcare and education. The destitute conditions of schools and clinics in the rural areas are the most eloquent testimony that the CPC has to work much harder here. In fact, its performance in social welfare for the rural population is worse than that in some ex-colonial countries.

There is a trend towards urbanization; villages in China are emptying of young people. The government should go about building towns and small cities for people leaving the villages. At the same time it should nudge businesses and industries to (re)locate to these new growing urban areas. Such urban planning is made all the more feasible with the existing highways and the train networks that are being constructed. This will not only reduce the pressure on big cities but will also lower the cost of doing business.

A more rational regional planning is part and parcel of the shift from investment-driven economic growth to a more consumption-driven economic growth. Well-planned urbanization not only improves the living conditions of the residents, it also increases efficiency in the use of public

---

[31] The housing problem in China, as in other countries, is not only an economic problem. It is also a serious social problem with ramifications for marriage amongst young people, family formation, work, etc.

[32] The literature on this is quite extensive. There is even a Wikipedia entry on it with many references: http://en.wikipedia.org/wiki/Chinese_property_bubble [accessed 27 June 2011].

[33] Bob Davis, "China Real-Estate Concerns Rise", *The Wall Street Journal*, 27 June 2011.

goods like schools and hospitals. Viewed from this perspective, such public expenditures can be seen as productive consumption. The end result is less social unrest, general uplifting of the skills base, a healthier workforce and greater social harmony, a goal that the CPC government has been claiming to achieve.

It is in the interest of the CPC to break the vicious cycle that has been feeding social unrest. However, to move from a vicious cycle to a virtuous cycle, a strong and committed leadership is indispensable. Just to be clear, a strong leadership does not mean oppression, surveillance and treating dissent as a crime. When the virtuous cycle kicks in, the huge expenses allocated for domestic security can be gradually reduced and the money used instead for goals like strengthening social safety nets.

To further support this position, a chapter from the history of the Soviet Union may be relevant. The Soviet Union disintegrated without a whimper. It happened not as a result of military defeat or civil war. In fact it collapsed with its police forces and military forces, including its nuclear weapon systems, fully intact. As is well-known now, the main reason was internal. Students of politics can easily see this as a poignant illustration of a new historical phenomenon: military strength has ceased to be a defining attribute of power.[34]

A high-level expression of China's economic strategy for the near future is contained in its five-year plan. It captures the intentions and concrete actions the Chinese leadership intends to pursue. It was formulated after long deliberations involving current and future leaders, various levels of government and business bodies. Barring unexpected major events, we can assume that the plan is the roadmap for Chinese economic development in the next few years.

The 12th Five-Year Plan*

On 14 March 2011 the National People's Congress approved the 12th Five-Year Plan (FYP) for China's economic and social development from 2011 to 2015. Compared to previous FYPs, this FYP deviates markedly in its target of development. Unlike past FYPs in which the absolute priority was economic growth, there is now more emphasis on ensuring and improving people's standards of living.

---

[34]John Lewis Gaddis, *The Cold War* (London: Penguin, 2005).
*This section first appeared as "China's 12th Five-Year Programme: Correct Targets But Questionable Measures" by Yang Mu in the *EAI Bulletin*.

Although there was a call to raise people's living standards in the 11th FYP, it was promoted under the concept of "Building a Harmonious Socialist Society". In the current plan, the call to improve people's lives has been given greater prominence. An interesting sign is the lowering of the target of annual GDP growth to 7 percent from 8 percent, previously the minimum growth rate needed to generate employment and maintain social stability. Economically, the one percentage point difference is negligible. What is crucial is the message for the people, especially the powerful Chinese officials who are the most important element in the implementation of the FYPs: the shift from the target of GDP growth to the improvement of people's lives.

There is also an urgency to reduce the income disparity, as evidenced in one of the 38 revisions to the 12th FYP made during the National People's Congress: from reducing the income gap step by step to reducing the income gap as soon as possible.

Among the raft of measures to address people's standards of living are increasing employment, improving workers' incomes, tackling poverty, increasing social security benefits, extending basic medical insurance coverage, promoting balanced population growth, and providing more affordable housing for low-income families.

What is unchanged is the traditional way of economic planning. First, the central government has set up detailed targets (including 12 binding targets and 12 guiding targets) to push local governments to change the targets of development, such as creating an extra 45 million urban jobs; raising per capita disposable income by an annual average of over 7 percent; providing affordable housing to around 20 percent of the urban households; and raising the proportion to over 70 percent of expenses for medical treatment paid out of the medical insurance fund.

Second is the high priority given to investment. After the stimulus package of 4 trillion yuan (end 2009 to 2011), over 10 trillion yuan has been earmarked in addition for developing seven strategic industries: 4 trillion yuan for infrastructure building in agriculture and irrigation; 4 trillion yuan for high-speed rail; and a few trillion yuan for government housing.

Third is the continued importance of state-owned enterprises and government-linked companies (GLCs). As in the past few years, most of the investments and bank loans will go to the SOEs or GLCs, which will continue to play important roles not only in traditional strategic industries such as energy and telecoms, but also in competitive industries such as coal mining, steel, food and property, which were supposedly left to private enterprises and the market in the economic reform period.

In sum, though the 12th FYP has set new targets, they are to be implemented using the old ways. The central and local governments, SOEs and investors play more important roles and are favoured in resource allocation and income distribution over the private sector, market and consumers. With the crucial mechanisms basically unchanged, it would be a wonder if people's lives are improved as quickly as the new FYP aims to achieve.

Concluding Remarks

When China embarked on its economic development in 1949, many people and well-wishers were hoping to see a new model of successful development. As a whole its record from the mid-1950s up to 1978 was not good, especially during the Cultural Revolution period. Since the reform in 1978, the performance of the Chinese economy has won much admiration. But has it charted a new direction for economic development? Has it provided new insights into modernization in the context of globalization? Some foreign observers have been so impressed by China's achievements that one of them has offered to capture the Chinese experience in a quasi-model which has come to be known as the Beijing Consensus. Interestingly, the Chinese leadership has shunned such claims.

China has been following the experiences of other East Asian countries, especially Japan. Looking ahead, the big challenge for China is to craft a set of workable policies that enable it to achieve sustainable economic development with social justice. The outside world would like to see China achieve power and wealth while contributing to global peace and prosperity. The insights gained are of great value to other rising powers (India, Brazil and Indonesia) because they face challenges similar to what confront China now.

To meet such a challenge, China needs to reinterpret old ideas and foreign experiences and adapt them to meet the needs of contemporary society, as well as to come up with fresh ideas. It is heartening to note that there are far-sighted intellectuals in China who care about such issues. For example, Yao Yang, Director of the China Center for Economic Research of Beijing University, says that for China to be taken seriously again by the international community, it must make contributions at the level of ideas. From the vantage point of human history, international competition is in the final analysis a competition of ideas.[35]

---

[35]姚洋, "是否存在一个中国模式?", 唐晋 (主编), 大国策: 经济模式 (北京: 人民出版社, 2009). (Yao Yang, "Is There a Chinese Model?", in Tang Jin (ed.), *Big Power Strategy: Economic Models* (Beijing: Renmin Publishing House, 2009), p. 63.)

Index